One to One

One to One
The Art of Conferring with Young Writers

∾

Lucy Calkins,
Amanda Hartman,
and Zoë White

HEINEMANN
Portsmouth, New Hampshire

Heinemann

A division of Reed Elsevier Inc.

361 Hanover Street

Portsmouth, NH 03801–3912

www.heinemann.com

Offices and agents throughout the world

Library of Congress Cataloging-in-Publication Data

Calkins, Lucy McCormick.

One to one : the art of conferring with young writers / Lucy Calkins,
Amanda Hartman, and Zoë White.

p. cm.

Includes index.

ISBN 0-325-00788-8 (alk. paper)

1. English language—Composition and exercises—Study and teaching
(Primary)—United States. 2. Creative writing (Primary education)—
United States. 3. Forums (Discussion and debate)—United States.
I. Hartman, Amanda. II. White, Zoë. III. Title.

LB1529.U6C35 2005

372.62′3—dc22   2004023639

Editor: Kate Montgomery

Production management: Sarah Weaver

Production coordination: Abigail M. Heim

Typesetter: Technologies 'N Typography

Interior design: Joyce Weston Design

Cover design: Lisa Fowler

Cover and interior photography: Peter Cunningham

Manufacturing: Louise Richardson

Printed in the United States of America on acid-free paper

08 07 06 05 04 RRD 1 2 3 4 5

Contents

Part Two: Conference Transcripts

Unit 6. *Nonfiction Writing: Procedures and Reports*

Unit 7. *Poetry: Powerful Thoughts in Tiny Packages*

Acknowledgments

This book stands on the shoulders of three decades of research and study done by the entire Teachers College Reading and Writing Project community. The book harvests ideas that grew from a close look at effective conferences. Some of those conferences were conducted by the coauthors of Units of Study for Primary Writing, and we are grateful to them: Leah Mermelstein, Abby Oxenhorn, Natalie Louis, Pat Bleichman, Laurie Pessah, and Stephanie Parsons. We are also grateful to Mary Ann Colbert and Linda Chen, who were important contributors to that series.

The Teachers College Reading and Writing Project participants have held a longstanding interest in conferring. We have learned tremendously from Donald Murray, whose writing conferences with me thirty years ago helped me understand that these one-to-one interactions are at the heart of teaching and learning writing. Our thinking also relies upon the eloquence and passion of Donald Graves, who brings the voices of children into all that we know about teaching writing. Our close colleague and friend, Carl Anderson, renewed our interest in conferring and set us on a road toward describing the kinds and components of effective conferences. His book, *How's It Going?* is a staple in our thought collaborative, and his generosity is legendary.

When a book has three coauthors, it is helpful to delineate the roles each has played. Zoë White is a marvelous writer, and she helped me to rewrite conferences and minilessons in the Units of Study for Primary Writing series. She has a special talent for making children come to life on the page, in all their quirkiness, and she helped bring kids to life in many of the conference transcripts. She is a kindergarten teacher, and she was the major writer in the first chapter and in the chapter about conferring in the content areas.

Amanda Hartman worked with me to study hundreds of conferences and deduce from them the principles that we name for you. She and I worked together to analyze kinds and methods of conferences—to see and name and clarify the moves a teacher can make within those conferences. Our process for writing this book, then, was first to collect transcripts of our conferences, then to analyze them and deduce guiding principles, then to return to the field and collect and record new conferences, and finally to revise conference transcripts to match the principles we'd outlined or inform new ones. In all of this work, Amanda led the way. Her role was to help all of us be sure that our teaching reflected our principles, and vice versa. Amanda is also an expert on working with English language learners; she had special responsibility for that chapter and for the chapter about the reading-writing connections in conferring.

This book really should have a fourth coauthor, for our editor, Kate Montgomery, functioned in ways that are far more important than one generally expects for an editor. We'd originally tucked all our thinking about conferring into the conference boldface headings themselves. Kate was the one to recognize that teachers would benefit if we explicitly addressed the intelligence behind those headings. She designed the structure for the book, rewrote a few of the chapters that were less than clear, selected these conferences, and rode herd on the entire process. Kate Montgomery has been the editor of the entire Units of Study for Primary Writing effort, and she is utterly irreplaceable. She is also one of the finest writers, teachers, and thinkers in the nation, and Heinemann is very lucky to have her as part of their team.

PART ONE

Understanding Conferring

∾

CHAPTER 1

The Essentials of Conferring with Young Writers

When teachers visit writing workshops at the Teachers College Reading and Writing Project, they often spend time trailing behind effective writing teachers, eavesdropping as those teachers move among their children. I wonder what the observers see. Does it seem that teachers of writing spend time chatting informally with children? I know the visitors see teachers draw a chair alongside one youngster, listen raptly, talk for a few minutes, laugh a bit . . . and then signal for the youngster to return to work, heading off to other children, perhaps to one who is sitting in a far corner of the room. To an outside observer, I suspect that conferring with young writers looks like No Big Deal.

But in the classrooms of some teachers, children grow in leaps and bounds, while in the classrooms of other teachers, children make only modest gains. I am utterly convinced that the difference has everything to do with the two teachers' abilities to confer. If a teacher can listen to a writer talk about her writing, and then can skim what the child has done so far and intervene in ways that lift the level not only of this piece of writing but of the child's work on future pieces, that teacher's conferences are a Very Big Deal. That teacher's children will learn to write in powerful ways.

When Zoë Ryder White, Amanda Hartman, and I first began work on this endeavor, we expected that teaching others to confer would be No Big Deal. We planned to transcribe lots of conferences and then to pop the transcripts into a book that would show how conferences do and do not change across the yearlong curriculum. After transcribing a few conferences, we sat down together to name the teaching moves we'd made and the principles that had guided us to choose those moves. We meant for that conversation to last an afternoon. Instead it has lasted eighteen months. We have revised those initial transcripts of conferences many times over, and in doing so, the three of us and our colleagues at the Teachers College Reading and Writing Project developed some model conferences. Then we took those model conferences back into classrooms. Now when we conferred, we kept the models in mind and often thought, "Is this suggesting that the model needs to be refined? Or that we need new models alongside the existing ones?" We've come to realize that learning to confer well is a Very Big Deal indeed!

The three of us have emerged from this work with a set of explicit principles that guide all our conferences (and most of our small-group strategy lessons and large-group minilessons) and also with a potent means for improving any teaching method we choose to examine.

I heartily recommend that anyone who wants to become skilled at some aspect of teaching begin transcribing, examining, and collaboratively rewriting that element of teaching. When Amanda, Zoë, and I transcribed what we thought were perfectly fine conferences, we gave ourselves the gift of a shared revisable draft—a concrete, improvable object where there had once been only fleeting thoughts. We could now pull close around those transcripts, asking, "How could we have done these even better?" and "What are we saying about effective conferences?" By writing and revising our conferences and our ideas about conferring, we've ratcheted up the level of our teaching. I have often said that when human beings write, we give ourselves the chance to put our thinking on the page, to hold our thinking in our hands, to put our thinking in a pocket and take it out another day. When we write, we can *think about our thinking* . . . and we can *think with others* about our thinking. That is exactly what Amanda, Zoë, and I have done in order to write this book. I hope this book, then, teaches you not only about conferring, but also about the importance of gathering with colleagues to record and then revise your best thinking about any one aspect of your teaching.

From this sort of cyclical process, Zoë, Amanda, and I have derived principles and methods that can make an extraordinary difference in classrooms. We know the methods can lift the level of teaching because this year, we and our colleagues at the Teachers College Reading and Writing Project have been fortunate enough to help thousands of teachers learn to confer. We have watched methods and principles of conferring be translated into practices, and we have seen the level of those practices skyrocket.

I used to think that conferring well relied on sheer talent. I figured that some lucky teachers "had the touch"; these were the teachers who could look at a piece of writing, listen to the writer and . . . presto! They'd know exactly what and how to teach. Others would look at a draft, listen to a writer, and think, "Geez . . . how can I help?"

Of course, I used to think the same of writing; some people had talent, others didn't. *Real* writers could sit down at the desk, take up the pen, and out would flow beautiful, brilliant words. The rest of us would produce lots of pedestrian stuff, dotted sometimes with little flashes of insight or grace. But time has passed, and by now, I have become one of those *real* writers, and so I can say with some authority that many of us writers produce lots of pedestrian stuff. Writers who become skilled are generally those who reread, assess, and rewrite . . . and do this day in and day out, year in and year out.

In a similar fashion, I have come to realize that even very experienced teachers of writing may look at a child's draft, listen to his or her descriptions of writing, and be unsure how to proceed. Although we feign being relaxed and clear, our brains are frantically running back and forth, trying to pick up a trail worth following. "Geez, how will I be able to help?" we think, praying the child will say something so that—presto!—the clouds will part and clarity will shine through. Often we proceed in conferences as if we are feeling our way in the dark, watching for signs to show whether the path we've chosen will prove to be a reasonable one.

Conferring is always a challenge, and teachers of writing are wise not to take their abilities to confer for granted. Don Murray, the Pulitzer Prize–winning writer who is known by many as the Father of the Writing Process, once said, "If you know how to respond to your students in conferences, watch out. If you know how to use literature as exemplar text, watch out. If you know what to say to help a student writer get better, watch out. Watch out lest you lose the pioneer spirit that has made this field a great one. Watch out lest you suffer a hardening of the ideologies."

This book can equip you to confer well and to be part of an endless process of learning to confer. In so doing, this book can give you a power chip that will vitalize your teaching forever, for that is what conferring can do. Conferring can give us the force that makes our minilessons and curriculum development and assessment and everything else more powerful. It gives us an endless resource of teaching wisdom, an endless source of accountability, a system of checks and balances. And, it gives us laughter and human connection—the understanding of our children that gives spirit to our teaching.

The Tone and Nature of a Writing Conference

All of my colleagues at the Teachers College Reading and Writing Project and I are releasing a DVD, *Big Lessons from Small Writers*, that accompanies this book and the series, Units of Study for Primary Writing. I recommend you watch the clips of conferring before reading this book. From these, I hope you gain an overall sense for the tone and relationships in a writing conference. You'll notice that conferences feel collegial. The teacher does not stand above the child, holding the child's paper, giving the child directions. Instead the teacher and the child sit side by side, the teacher at the child's eye level. The child holds the writing and does most (or at least a lot of) the talking. The teacher may start the conversation by asking a broad question. The child responds, and the teacher listens closely, fascinated. The teacher often responds just a bit to the content of child's work. "Oh, I didn't know you had a new baby in your family, how exciting!" or, "I'm sorry to hear your dad is away. I bet you miss him." The teacher probably asks a question or two to extend what the child has said or shown. Then the conference seems to turn a corner; now the teacher will explicitly teach one thing and help the child get started integrating this new skill or strategy into her ongoing writing work.

Conference Architecture

Most of us do not realize that our interactions with other people at times follow a predictable structure, but this is nevertheless the case. In traditional classrooms, for example, the teacher will often ask a question, elicit a response from a student, and then evaluate that response. For instance, the teacher asks, "What is the capital of New York?" The child responds, "Albany." The teacher assesses, saying, "Very good."

This pattern of interaction doesn't often occur outside of classrooms. Usually, if a person asks, "What is the capital of New York State?" and learns that it is Albany, the response would be, "Thanks," not "Very good." Teachers who follow this question-response-evaluate pattern of interaction may not realize they are doing so. These teachers may think they are utterly changing their teaching when, for example, they work with new content (asking questions about history instead of geography) or when they ask questions that require analysis rather than simply fact recall. But the truth is that as long as the pattern of interaction in such teaching remains the same, the instruction itself will convey many of the same messages—that knowledge is in the teacher's hands, to be selected, parceled out, and judged by her rather than weighed, shared, and investigated with her.

When a teacher confers with a writer, her interactions tend to follow a consistent pattern, one that teachers of writing have deliberately chosen. This pattern is not unlike the pattern one would see between a doctor and a patient, a client and her hairdresser, or a car owner and a mechanic—it's one common to many human interactions. We've named the steps *research, decide, teach,* and *link*.

Research

Observe and interview to understand what the child is trying to do as a writer. Probe to glean more about the child's intentions.

When we bring our car in for servicing, the car mechanic doesn't just dive under the hood and begin yanking out wires, changing gaskets, and draining fluids. Instead, the mechanic asks us how the car has been driving lately. In the same way, a doctor will not begin treating a patient or even looking for physical signs of ailment before asking the patient to describe the situation in his or her own words. "How have you been feeling?" the doctor might ask, knowing that the patient's description will be crucial to making an accurate diagnosis. Similarly, a writing conference usually begins with the teacher asking, "How's your writing work going?" or "What have you been working on as a writer?"

Because young children may not have learned to articulate exactly what they are trying to do as writers—and may not, in fact, be aware of trying to do *anything*—the research component of conferences with beginning writers often involves watching what the child is doing, looking at the paper to understand what the child has done, and naming what it is that the child seems to be trying to do as a writer. "I can tell you have added a lot of excitement. You have a whole lot of exclamation marks, don't you!" we might say. Often our research involves double-checking hunches we develop from looking at the child's work. "It looks to me like you are in the midst of rereading your writing. Are you checking to make sure it makes sense?" we might ask. Or "I see that you are drawing pictures that show exactly what happened in your story about the beach."

We might even put words to what the child has done that he would probably not use himself. "Wow, it looks like you stretched your story out across three whole pages and now you are going back to add labels!" We don't really expect the child to explain the work in this way, but we do know that when we articulate what we think the child has done and what we anticipate he may want to do next, we are demonstrating for children the ways we hope they will eventually be able to talk about their writing.

Of course, when we study the evidence and say to the writer, "It looks like you have two drafts here," there will be times when the author lets us know that we have it all wrong. "No, these are not two drafts . . . they are two *chapters* of my story," the child may point out.

Once children have been in a writing workshop for a few months, they become skilled at responding to our research questions. When we ask, "What have you been working on as a writer?" five- and six-year-old children will respond, "Well, I was trying to write this as a small-moment story, but actually it got too big. So now I am trying to decide if I should write a new story or if I should make this one smaller." Typically, we respond by making sure we understand. "Can you show me? What do you mean your story got too big?" we ask. We might well ask this question even if we know what the child's words mean but want to learn what they mean to the child. Our focus is on trying to understand the writer's perceptions, intentions, and plans. When we do, we are able to tailor our teaching so that it will help writers grow just beyond where they are able to grow on their own—into their zones of proximal development.

Name what the child has already done as a writer and remind the child to do this in future writing.

Because our goal as teachers is to bring our students as far as possible along the writing path, and because we know that each conference is a precious opportunity to teach only one of the myriad teaching points available, we sometimes get fixated on the many things the child does not yet know how to do. We want to study what the child is doing (or not doing) in order to decide what new thing to teach—but our conferences will in fact be more successful and meaningful if we look for the child's successes as well as for teaching opportunities.

As we research, we need to look for and then name something that the child has done well—a valuable piece of the writing process that we want to encourage the child to always use. Even if the thing we notice was not necessarily done intentionally, our attention to and naming of the act or process will reveal it to be a useful writing skill. "I am noticing," we might say, "that you are rereading what you wrote before adding more words—that is so smart of you. Writers do that all the time!" Or "I love how you put so much detail into that picture of you and your cousin at the top of the Ferris wheel—I can even see your hair blowing in the wind! Writers do that, you know, add as much detail as they can into their writing so their readers can know even more about their stories."

The challenge for us as teachers is to notice a very specific way in which the child has succeeded, and then to phrase a compliment in such a way that the child knows it is something she should carry into her writing work in general.

Decide

Weigh whether you want to accept or alter the child's current plans and processes. Decide what you want to teach and how you will teach it.

This next component of a writing conference is not one that takes place in the open but quietly, in the mind of the teacher. As we are researching and learning about the child's processes, our minds are busy searching through all that we know about writing and all that we know about the particular child in order to pinpoint what we can teach that will make the biggest impact on the child as a writer—not only in this instance but in the child's writing life as a whole. We ask ourselves, "What can I teach this child that he can immediately begin incorporating into today's work, but that also is a skill or process he will be able to draw on with independence in subsequent writing?"

There is no one right answer to this question. Our teaching decisions are influenced by a variety of factors. The more we learn about teaching writing, the more options we can consider, and imagining options allows us to tailor our teaching to the needs of each student during each conference. The decision should definitely be influenced by the child's intention. That is, a given piece of writing could presumably be improved in dozens of different ways. If the child has already decided he wants to show rather than tell his excitement at winning a trophy, then rather than teaching the child to develop his characters, we would be wise to use a strategy that equips the child to do what he has already decided to do. We must also take the curriculum into account. If we are trying to launch a unit of study on authors as mentors, then it is likely that we'll teach that child to show, not tell, by highlighting a place in a book where a published author has done that. At the beginning of a new unit, especially, the curriculum is influential in our decision of which teaching point to choose because it is through individual conferring that we actually build the class' enthusiasm for the work of the new unit. Then, too, our decisions are influenced by our assessments of each child. Although the class may be working on learning from authors, a particular child may not yet read with one-to-one correspondence, and we may have decided that during writing as well as reading time, we need to support these foundational reading-writing behaviors. During the research phase of a conference, then, we consider a variety of possible teaching points and decide on one.

As we make a decision about *what* to teach, we also think about *how* we will teach. We must determine which of several effective teaching methods will be best suited to a particular teaching point and a particular student. As we decide, we weigh whether we will teach by *guided practice,* by *demonstration,* by *explaining and showing an example,* or by *inquiry.* Each of these methods is discussed more thoroughly later in this chapter. In general, primary writing conferences tend to rely on guided practice.

Teach

Help the child get started doing what you hope he or she will do. Intervene to lift the level of what the child is doing.

Once we have decided what we will teach, a conference resembles a minilesson. It's helpful for the child if we come right out and say what we will teach. Often, we can also connect what we will teach to the child's ongoing work, explaining how we came to decide upon this one teaching point. We might say, "I have been watching you work so hard on spelling every one of your words, saying each word slowly and putting down the sounds you hear. It is really smart the way you say your words sl—o—w—ly, like a turtle. But today I want to teach you that writers also have some words they spell fast-like-a-rabbit." The start of the teaching component in a conference correlates with the "connection" phase of a minilesson.

There are several effective methods people can use to teach writers. In every conference and every minilesson, a teacher will use either *guided practice, demonstration, explicitly telling and showing an example,* or (occasionally) *inquiry.* In the conferences in this book, you will notice that the teaching method is noted.

It is helpful to realize that, once we have decided upon the method we will use for a particular teaching point, the conference unfolds in a fairly predictable fashion. Kids are always utterly unpredictable, of course, but each of the teaching methods we incorporate into our conferences (and minilessons) has a predictable plot line. We hope you'll come to internalize the way demonstration conferences, for example, tend to go because you will read some within the pages of this book, and because you will see that each demonstration conference is built around a predictable set of guidelines. This means that if you decide your teaching method will be demonstration, you should have a sense for the main moves your teaching will take, and those main moves will be highlighted in the transcripts with bold guidelines.

As our conferring skills improve, we will be more flexible in imagining how any one teaching point could be taught using any one of the four major methods of teaching. Although these are all possible methods, two of them will be especially useful when teaching very young children to do things—and this is true whether we are teaching cooking or swimming or writing—*demonstration* and *guided practice.*

Teaching Method: Demonstration

One common method of teaching in primary writing conferences is *demonstration.* If I want to teach a very little child to make pancakes, for example, I am not going to be very effective if I stand in the front of a classroom explaining, "Wait until the bottom of the first side is golden brown and the bubbles on the top of the pancake have started to pop." Instead, I am going to bring in an electric frying pan or bring the student of pancakes next to the stove, and then I will show the child how to cook pancakes. "See, the bottom here is beginning to get golden," I might say, lifting up an edge of one pancake with a spatula for her to see. "That's how you decide if a pancake is ready to flip." Now, although my conference is a demonstration one, I shift to guided practice (which is usually a part of a demonstration conference). Handing the child the spatula, I offer a quick coaching tip. "You peek under the next one. That's it. Slide it under. Does it look brown?" Then we'll be ready for the next step, and again, I may demonstrate with my pancake. Soon I'll be debriefing, "Did you see how I slid the spatula under about half the pancake, then flipped it? You try it."

Teaching writing by demonstration is not very different from my lesson in pancake cooking. If we decide to demonstrate, we will show the child exactly what we mean for her to do later on her own. We sometimes demonstrate by showing the child what we do on our own writing, and we sometimes temporarily take over a tiny bit of the child's piece so that we can use it for our demonstration. Then we get the writer started doing whatever we have demonstrated, and we coach her efforts just as we did when she stood with spatula in hand. "That's it. Now you need to . . ." we say.

For example, if I want to teach a student that writers who have a lot to say write their words in a sentence at the bottom of the page, I might say, "Let me show you how writers with a lot to say in their stories—like you—write their words in a sentence at the bottom of the page. What do you want to write?" If the child says, "Today I will ride my bike . . ." I might decide to use the first word as a place to demonstrate. "Watch how I say 'Today' and listen for the sounds," I say. "To-day. To, /t/, /t/ . . ." and then I write the *t*, reread it, and continue to say the word *today*. Then I debrief. "Did you see how I said the word, listened to the first sound, wrote it down, and then reread it? Can you do the same with the next word?"

Teaching Method: Guided Practice

The other common method of teaching in primary writing conferences is *guided practice.* Just as we teach a child to swim by physically getting into the pool and showing her how to breath and move, we use guided practice in writing conferences to scaffold the child as, with our support, she tries what we hope she will soon be able to do on her own. As we move into the teaching phase of the conference, we name for the child what we will teach. We try to explain that the thing we'll teach is something all writers do, all the time. For example, we might say, "When writers are writing words, they say the word, listen to the sounds they hear, and then write those sounds down on the paper." Then we interject the first of many lean prompts, this one designed to get the child started: "Say the word." The child will. Next we continue giving brief directives designed either to scaffold the child's work in a step-by-step fashion or to lift the level of the child's work. Once the child has attempted the new work with this scaffolding, we will let the intervals between prompts become longer, or omit some of the prompts to allow the child to continue working with less support. Finally, as in every conference, we name what the writer has done and remind her to do this often in future writing.

Teaching Methods: Explicitly Tell and Show an Example; Inquiry

Another common teaching method is to *explicitly tell and show an example.* Often when using this method, we feel as if we are giving a short speech to the child. The trick is to make the speech memorable. One way to do this is to use a metaphor. "Writers don't write about big watermelon topics," we might say, gesturing to show the hugeness of a watermelon. "We don't write 'all-about-our-summer.' Instead we write about tiny seed ideas, like about swimming in the creek and seeing a water spider tiptoe across the water's surface." Often we bring home our point by referencing our own writing or the writing done by a published author or another child. For instance, we might describe a peer who started out with a huge topic like "my mom," then worked on zooming in, and wrote a focused story about just one time with Mom, perhaps about "when we got ice cream and ate it on our favorite bench in the park. It was so hot the ice cream melted down our wrists." Finally, as with the other methods, we encourage the child to try out the new strategy; we name what he or she has done; and we remind the child to do this often in future writing.

The fourth teaching method, *inquiry,* is not one that is used often in the primary writing workshop as it relies on a level of sophistication that is usually found only in more experienced writers. When using inquiry to teach, we invite the student to study something with us, and we help the student extrapolate from the example principles that she could apply to her own writing.

No matter which teaching method we use in a conference, the most important part of our teaching occurs when we stop teaching and say to the child, "Now you try it."

Link

Name what the child has done as a writer and remind the child to do this often in the future.

At the end of every conference, we name what the child has learned and done—referring back, of course, to what we told the child we'd be teaching at the beginning of the conference. We essentially give a second compliment, only this time we are complimenting the new work the child has done. We again remind the child that it will be important to continue doing this good work often in future writing pieces. An explicit link helps the child transfer what we have taught today into his independent writing process.

Kinds of Conferences

Although most conferences follow roughly the same architecture, there are three main kinds of conferences, each with a slightly different focus: *content conferences, expectations conferences,* and *process and goals conferences.*

Content Conferences

Especially at the beginning of the year, many of the conferences we have with young writers will be *content conferences* in which we hope to elicit richer, more detailed and complete stories. Either a teacher or a peer can function as an encouraging presence in the conference. As we listen, we interject quiet comments that prompt the writer to say more. "Oh my goodness, what a huge sandcastle!" we might say. "How did you build it?" We might retell or repeat what the child has said to us, not only giving the child a sense of her own story, but encouraging her to add even more to the end—"So then what happened?" we might prompt. When the writer has generated a lot of detail, our role is to encourage the child to record on paper what she has said. "Wow, I had no idea you put real shells around the edges of the castle. That sounds beautiful! You *have* to put that on your paper so all of your readers know about it!" Because this involves adding on, we must often then teach the child a strategy for recording the new information. Perhaps the writer must staple on a new sheet of paper to continue the story, or perhaps she must add more details to the picture she has begun. Perhaps she has added so much to her original story that she must start an entirely new draft.

Expectation Conferences

Especially when we have just launched the writing workshop, we must also use our conferences to teach children how writing workshop goes—the expectations we hold for writers in our classroom writing community. *Expectation conferences* are generally precipitated by a child who shows us that he has not yet settled into the routines of the writing workshop. It is usually quite easy to recognize a situation that calls for this kind of conference: The child is walking around the room instead of sitting and writing; the child is using writing as a motor activity rather than attempting to communicate a message; the child is arguing over a particular chair with another child. In these instances, we may cut out the research phase of the conference and begin by letting the child know explicitly, firmly, and with warmth that what he is doing does not match our expectations for behavior during writing workshop. Sometimes, especially at the beginning of the year, children are not being intentionally or willfully disruptive; they simply must be taught and then reminded of the expectations for writing time and for writers. Once we have gotten the child on a more productive track, we might continue with another kind of conference related to the child's writing work.

Process and Goals Conferences

As our young writers progress, we find ourselves more often having *process and goals conferences*. At one point we believed that this kind of conference was actually two types, a process conference and a goals conference, but we found that most often these conferences contain a mix of both. For example, you might want to teach a child that writers sometimes add sound effects into their writing just like

Donald Crews does (a goals conference), but then you will probably want to teach the child how to go about doing that today and often in her writing work (process conference). Or you may decide to teach the child how to add a flap onto her story to fit more words on the page (process); then you will also want to teach the child that writers sometimes revise their stories in order to add more details (goals). Especially because we are teaching young children, we have found that it is important to make a connection between the more abstract goals we teach as part of the writing process (write with details) and strategies the child can use to incorporate that goal into his or her own writing (using carets to insert more specifics).

While there is a clear distinction between each of the kinds of conferences we have discussed here, the great majority of primary conferences throughout the year will be process and goals conferences.

This year, I've learned the power of conferring from the inside. In September, charged with leading what has now become a very large organization, I decided to give myself the gift of a leadership coach. And so for half an hour a week, I talk on the phone with Ellen Fredericks, my coach. The conversations have been warm and informal. If you were to listen in, you might think we were just two friends, talking over my work—you might think it to be No Big Deal. But in fact, Ellen has put me through my paces, instructing me in deliberate and highly planned ways, taking me through a course of self-improvement. And our half-hour-a-week conversations stay with me day in and day out, all week long.

My coach often asks me: What's your ultimate goal? What positive steps forward could you take? What's getting in your way of taking those steps? Who do you need to talk with or what do you need to do in order to get the help you need? The questions are good ones, but I know that half of her gift lies not in what she does, but in what she's taught me I need to do because of our appointments to talk. She makes me choose goals, prioritize, plan, imagine alternatives, set a deliberate course, assess, reflect on my own role, take actions . . . she makes me learn from my own experiences. I want all our children, indeed, all of us, to have opportunities to do the same.

It is not easy to confer with people—grownups or children—for little bits of time, and yet to have those interactions alter the person's perspectives and work for evermore. But this is what we are called to do when we confer.

CHAPTER 2

⤳

The Management That Makes Conferring Possible

As educators from more and more school systems adopt the reading and writing workshop models for literacy instruction, one of the most pressing concerns many teachers have is how to structure the classroom and the teaching day to support plentiful, constructive conferring. In school after school, teachers have asked us to come into their classrooms and show them the management "magic" that makes one-to-one conferring possible.

Teachers who ask for this assistance demonstrate their knowledge of the writing workshop. They are right that the one-to-one conference is an essential part of this approach to teaching writing. In fact, in Australia, the writing workshop approach was for many years known as the "conference" approach to teaching writing. Teachers who ask for help managing their classrooms so that conferring is possible need to know that the first secret to a well-managed writing workshop is to improve the writing instruction we give to children. I trust that the Units of Study for Primary Writing series is helping teachers to do just that. But in addition, teachers need to institute practices that support children working with enough independence that the teachers are free to teach.

Specifically, teachers need to learn to do the following three things to provide the children with classroom contexts in which frequent, powerful one-to-one conferring is possible. We need to:

- Equip students to cycle through each day's workshop and through the writing process with independence.

- Anticipate predictable problems that will occur during writing time; identify and analyze unpredicted problems in order to devise long-term solutions.

- Develop management structures that support conferring.

- Balance one-to-one conferring with small-group work.

Equip Students to Work with Independence

To equip students to work with independence during each day's workshop and the writing process, we need to:

- Imagine a writing process that is within the grasp of each child. This means our goals and instruction need to be multileveled.

- Plan a writing workshop in great detail so that we and our students learn to proceed efficiently, even automatically.

- Teach children to start writing without needing an individualized jump-start.

- Teach children to sustain themselves as writers, to figure out what to do when they are stuck and to shift between writing, revising, and starting a new piece.

Imagine a Writing Process That Is Within the Grasp of Each Child

A teacher can hold one-to-one conferences with individual students only if most children in the class are able to carry on with some independence. When I tell this to teachers of primary-level students, the teachers often respond with a perplexed look. "But, but . . . but my kids are five years old! They need me for so many things," they often say, adding, "I *definitely* don't have the kind of class that will allow me to confer quietly with individuals while the rest of the class works independently."

None of our classes enter the year able to sustain independent writing. But all of them can achieve this goal. We simply need to teach children how to proceed with independence through the writing process and throughout the writing workshop.

Before the first three weeks of the school year are over, almost every child can learn to cycle through the entire writing process independently. That is, by the end of September, almost every child should be able to choose his or her subject, plan the writing, write, and then revise by adding more information without needing to check in with the teacher.

Of course, this is possible only if we widen our image of "cycling through the process" so that we imagine a process that is within easy grasp of every child. A five-year-old child with no knowledge of letter-sound correspondence can move independently through the writing process if that process involves remembering something she has done; making a movie in her mind of that event; drawing a picture that captures the story on the page; writing the story as best she can (if she can); rereading and thinking, "What else happened?" and then drawing or writing to add detail. Of course, we soon want children to do more than this, but our expectations should never be so high that children can only do the work with step-by-step help from an adult.

The goals we envision and the instruction we provide need to be multileveled. The good news for a primary writing workshop: It is not hard to provide for multileveled work. The secret lies in differentiated materials. Once we discern what is within the grasp of each child, we set each child up to write on paper that is "just right" for him. This means that we need to duplicate paper in a variety of formats so that some children write on four-page booklets that have ten lines on each page while others write on four-page booklets that have two lines on each page. The varied paper reflects varied expectations. Some children will retell an event using just the broad strokes while others will elaborate with dialogue, details, inner thoughts, and more. But all children can remember something they have done, draw the events across the pages of their booklets, and then represent the story as best they can.

When we say that children need to be able to progress through the writing process with independence, our goal is not for teachers to step aside. Instead, our goal is instruction resembling that of a basketball coach. The players on a basketball team know how to play the game and do not need moment-to-moment instructions from the coach in order to carry on. This frees the coach to observe and choose when to intervene to teach. Likewise, kids need to be able to progress through the writing process with independence not so we can stop teaching, but so we are more free to teach. While kids hum along, writing as best they are able, we can step in to scaffold, helping one particular child or group of children for a few minutes, but then stepping aside and letting that child or group return to approximating writing with independence while we watch from afar, readying ourselves to intervene with another child or cluster of children.

When we teach toward independence it means that we hold our teaching accountable to making a lasting difference long after we have left the child's side. In conferences, minilessons, and small-group strategy lessons, our goal is to intervene in a way that *lifts the level of what kids do independently*. This means, of course, that we need to relinquish any notion that any one teaching interaction will help a child leapfrog his or her way to vastly more mature work. If we try to help a child who is labeling her drawing with initial and final consonants write words such as *because* correctly, the chances are good she won't be able to continue doing what we have taught her with any independence. We might, however, be successful if we try to teach such a child that after she has labeled many parts of her drawing, it is helpful to go back and reread what she has written, putting her finger under her letters as she rereads.

Plan the Proceedings of a Writing Workshop in Detail

It is important to plan the proceedings of a writing workshop in great detail so that both we and our students learn to proceed through the workshop automatically and efficiently. If the first secret to a successful workshop is to tailor our teaching and expectations so they are within each child's independent grasp, the second secret is to plan not only our teaching but also our children's independent work. Just as many brides think through every step of their weddings, imagining where the guests will enter, how they'll move through the space, and what signals will cue participants to progress to the next events, so, too, do teachers need to think about how their students will move independently through every step of the writing workshop.

Before a teacher even launches a writing workshop, it is important for the teacher to mentally inch through the chronological sequence of the workshop. For example, a teacher might ask herself these questions (and others) while she plans just the first fifteen minutes of her workshop:

- When I want to gather children for the minilesson, how will I signal to them to stop what they are doing, look at me, and be ready to listen to my instructions? Presumably I will use the same method every day to recruit their attention, but what will it be?

- Will I want children to bring their work with them when they gather in the meeting area, or to set their work out at their work spots before convening? If they bring their work, will I want them to lay their writing folders on the floor in front of them, to sit on them, or what?

- How will I gather children efficiently and smoothly? Will I call them by table? Will I ask them to push in their chairs? What will I do if they dawdle? Will they need to step over each other as they arrive in the meeting area or can that be avoided?

- How will children sit? Will there be assigned seats in the meeting area? Rows? Will I put specific children up front, within reach of a quieting hand? Will my paraprofessional (or parent assistant) sit in the midst of the group? Will the children sit cross-legged, on their bottoms, hands in their laps, and if so, how will I describe that particular way of sitting when I want to remind them to take these positions?

- What will I expect the first children who arrive in the meeting area to do while they wait for everyone to gather? Will they sing a gathering song? Talk among themselves? Read poems or messages that I'll post for this purpose?

- When children turn and talk in minilessons, will they have assigned partners already in place? What will children do if their partner is absent?

- When it is time for children to turn and talk during the meeting, how will I signal them to turn their attention back to me? Will this be the signal I will use before gathering them for a mini-lesson?

- If some children are confused by the minilesson or do not know how to get started on writing, how will I know this and provide them with the support they need early on in the writing work-shop? Will I have a predictable way of discerning which children are ready to work and which need more support or direction? After dispersing the others, will I regularly keep a cluster of children with me in the meeting area so I can provide the small group with more direction? Alternatively, will I spend the first five minutes researching as children get started, then convene a small group together to provide them with more support?

- How will I send children from the meeting areas to their places without a traffic jam? Will table monitors get the table supplies first? Will I dismiss one table at a time from the meeting area?

- When I send children off to write, what exactly do I envision each child will do during the transition from sitting in the meeting area to writing?

- Where will the writing paper be kept so that children can access it whenever they need more? How will this area be maintained?

You may be skeptical. Can I really plan in such a microfashion? Isn't this over the top? Can teachers really think through such a host of logistical questions in order to teach just the first fifteen minutes of a writing workshop? My answer is that this sort of planning is *exactly* what you need to do. Remember that you are planning not for one day but for *every day, every year,* and that many of your plans will support reading as well as writing. If you plan and teach and supervise your children so that every day, they gather in the meeting area smoothly (for example), this will come back to bless you every day.

It is crucial that you use minilessons and midworkshop teaching points as occasions to explicitly teach children how you expect them to proceed during a writing workshop. I encourage you to notice how Leah and I did this during the *Launching the Writing Workshop* unit in our series, and prepare to invent your own ways to streamline the logistics that need to be addressed in your class. For example, if you want kids to be more efficient, you can focus on this by saying, "Writers definitely want to make sure they don't waste precious moments of the writing workshop. Let me show you how we. . . ."

Although I have focused so far on the first fifteen minutes of the writing workshop, it is important to plan every minute of the workshop with similar care. Once kids have been sent off to work on their own, their needs change. Now we need to plan (and teach) so that children proceed with independence through the writing process.

Teach Children to Start Writing Without an Individualized Jump Start

In thinking through children's writing processes, it is reasonable to start at the very beginning. The first challenge is to teach children that they can get themselves started on their writing each day. That is, after the minilesson ends, it is crucial that children do not rely on receiving an individualized jump start. We need to resist the temptation to move quickly through the classroom, setting paper out in front of each individual, asking each child, "What will you write?" and then saying, "So put that down right here . . . get started." Instead, we need to explicitly teach children that writers can get started on their own.

For example, when children are still gathered around us on the carpet, we can say to them, "Would you give me a thumbs up if you know what you are going to write? How many of you can picture yourself going to your writing spot and getting started and doing this entirely *on your own!*" Then, after individuals have signaled that they feel confident they can be self-starters, we might say, "So Raymond and Tanya, why don't you show us how you go straight to your writing spot and get started *all by yourselves.* The rest of us will admire you as you do this." As the two head off, we can act like sportscasters, chronicling their every move. "Oh, look, they've opened their folders all by themselves and gotten their writing out and put those folders away, too. Isn't that grown up of them! My goodness, I can't believe my eyes. It looks like Raymond is rereading what he already wrote, just like fourth graders do. . . ."

After a few days of releasing children from the carpet in small clusters, only after they've formed a clear image of exactly what they will do to begin writing, we may graduate to the point where we send whole tables of kids to get started on their writing. Now we may decide to move from table to table, clipboard in hand, saying, "I'm just watching and admiring and recording which kids are able to get started on their own. Oh! Look! Jeremy has already started sketching his new story. That's a smart way to begin." Alternatively, if it seems warranted, we may provide an additional scaffold for self-starting, asking children to record their progress each day on a checklist of things they need to do to start writing on their own. Such a checklist would be helpful for a few days, and then—like training wheels— could be removed.

Once we have let children know that we are on the lookout for those who are self-starters, our support for self-starting can probably become mostly nonverbal. Approaching one child, we may simply gesture toward the child's pencil. For another child, we may gesture to the page, or touch our lips to indicate that it's time to turn from talking to working. These nonverbal cues are important because they insure that our efforts to manage the class don't create their own waves of chaos and because these teaching interventions let children feel as if they are self-monitoring.

"But what if this isn't enough?" you might ask. If children need more help getting started on each day's writing, then we may decide to give minilessons in which we explicitly teach strategies for doing this. We could, for example, teach children that one way writers get started is to reread and reexamine whatever they did yesterday, think- ing, "Is there anything I can add on to what I have already done?" Then, too, we can give minilessons in which we teach writers that their first job each day is to decide what they will do, giving them- selves a self-assignment. Then their next job is to set up their work- space so they can write. In such a minilesson, we can teach the class that if one writer decides she is going to write a new story, she needs to put away the old pieces (deciding a piece is finished without confirmation from her teacher), get new paper, and start writing. Of course, the minilessons we give will vary based on our assessment of the problem. If we think that the children delay getting started because they think they need a teacher to help them choose topics to write about, we will give minilessons on choosing topics for writing.

We may decide that only a subset of the class needs explicit help learning to become self-starters, in which case, after teaching the day's minilesson, we can ask that group to remain in the meeting area. Instead of helping each one of these kids individually, we can provide the group with a strategy lesson. For example, these children might have a chart of instructions to follow, and we could read the chart with them, watching as they do each step.

Teach Children to Sustain Themselves as Writers

It invariably happens that three minutes after kids have started writing, they tell us they are done. One by one, they come up to us. "I'm finished!" one child says. "Here's my story!" another says. The unstated question is, "What should I do next?" We must teach children to figure out what to do as they shift between writing, revising, and starting a new piece—how to sustain the writing process.

The crucial thing to remember is that if a child has the strategies to start writing, then at the very least, that child has the wherewithal to finish one piece and start another. So it is safe to respond to the child who seems unable to get past "I'm done," by saying, "I *know* you can figure out what to do next!" If the child needs more help, we can spell it out. "When writers finish one story, they start the next one! You know how to get started writing a story, don't you? The first thing you need to do is to think [and now, the initiating question varies a bit depending on whether you hope kids are writing narratives or non-narratives], 'What have I done recently that I could write about?' or 'What's important to me that I could tell about?'"

Sometimes a teacher feels kids will write quickly and sloppily if the teacher does not function as a full-time manager. The teacher feels he needs to intervene to promote revision and craftsmanship. "I tell kids they need to check with me before they can decide they are done," these teachers say. This is certainly understandable, but if many children in the class are racing through pieces of writing, the most efficient way to address this is through minilessons. We can pull the children together and teach them that writers have a saying: "When you're done, you've just begun." We can showcase children who finished a draft and then reread, adding more, and we can tell the class that those children are writing just like published authors. Some children will still whip through one piece after the next, but the truth is that no great harm results from this. And if we relinquish the role of monitor in order to confer with writers, those conferences give us the forum we need to help these children develop an understanding of revision.

You are right to sputter, "But, but . . . don't we want them to . . . ?" You can fill in the final word of that sentence. Don't we want them to write with print as well as pictures, to spell more conventionally, to add on, to revise their endings, and so forth? All of these are worthy goals. But the truth of the matter is that the best way to support children learning to do more with some independence is through conferences. And we can't conduct writing conferences unless kids can carry on independently, cycling through the writing process. So sometimes, we need to lessen our attachment to all sorts of worthy goals in order to have the opportunities to teach toward these goals.

For example, we absolutely *do* want children to spell as conventionally as they can and to revise. But at the start of the year, it is likely that a large percentage of the class will be writing a bunch of undeveloped pieces within each hour-long writing workshop while we move among the kids, teaching one and then another and another to stretch out words and record the sounds they hear, use sight words as they write, revise for detail and focus, and so on. Once we have taught children these skills through conferences and small-group strategy lessons and celebrated those who use these techniques with our support or, better yet, on their own, the level of what children are able to do on their own will rise. Within a few months, many children will independently draft, revise, and edit their writing. If they don't, once we've taught toward these goals in one-to-one conferences, it's easier for us to make a whole-class fuss about this, saying, for example, "I don't want any of you to write one-day pieces anymore. You all know how to spend a few days rather than a few minutes working on a piece, and to revise your own writing before coming to me saying, 'I'm done.'"

Address Predictable and Unpredictable Problems

On the last day of the Teachers College Reading and Writing Project's summer institute, I sometimes tell teachers that the one thing I know for certain is that when they go back to their classrooms and try to put everything they learn at the institute in place, things won't work. When any of us launches a writing workshop, the one thing we can know for certain is that there will be problems. Struggling writers will spend forever at the pencil sharpener, until their pencils are stubs. Others will wander the room, looking for topics or paper or excuses for not working. Writing folders will brim with illegible work. Children will interrupt our carefully planned minilessons to report they have new sneakers, or to tell about a dot of blood they've found under a fingernail. Children will spend more time drawing intricate decorations onto their characters' dresses than recording their stories.

The important thing for teachers to know is that these problems will always occur, and problems don't mean the writing workshop is a failure, and they don't mean that you and your kids aren't genetically wired for this sort of instruction. It helps a lot if you:

- Anticipate predictable problems and rehearse mentally how you'll respond.

- Anticipate that unpredicted problems will also occur. Give yourself time to study those problems and to invent long-term solutions.

Anticipate Predictable Problems and Rehearse Your Response

We benefit enormously from having a plan for how we'll respond to the inevitable problems in teaching. When we imagine how minilessons will proceed in our classrooms, we need to also imagine the children who will interrupt our teaching to ask, "Can I sharpen my pencil?" Then we can rehearse how we will respond, keeping in mind that when we respond to one child, we are teaching others as well. "Mario," I might say, "I am confused. You are asking *now*, in the middle of a *minilesson*, whether you can sharpen your pencil? This is a minilesson; this is an important time for you to be listening." That is, we need to socialize Mario into the norms of the community by showing him (and all his classmates) what we expect. "If there is a life-or-death reason why that pencil must be sharpened at this exact moment, you need to explain that to me, Mario, because otherwise I don't really understand why you'd interrupt our precious minilesson time to talk about sharpening a pencil." This may sound harsh; a warm tone can soften the message, but it is kinder to come on strong *once* rather than harping on the same issue a hundred times.

Then, too, we can rehearse for the predictable situation that some children will become too reliant on us. From the start of the school year, we can predict that some kids will try to rely on us to tell them what to do at every step of the way. We can, from the start, get out of the business of telling writers what to do next. Mental alarms should go off if children are coming up to us at every step. Something is wrong if we need to signal to children that, yes, they can add one more page, or yes, they can put work in the finished pocket or yes, they can get new paper or leave a blank for a word they can't spell. We can, in each of these instances, teach kids to make their own decisions. If a child approaches one of us with her story in hand, saying, "I'm done!" with the intonation that suggests she is also asking, "What should I do next?" we are wise to say, "Nice job. You know what to do next, don't you?" Of course, the child might not pick up on our nudge, and we may end up reminding her of what she can do when she finishes a piece. However, we definitely want to teach this in such a way that another time, the child can make this decision on her own. Similarly, if a child comes to us, asking, "Can I get more paper?" our wisest response is to say, "I bet you can figure out what to do, can't you? Do you see, you can solve your own problems!"

When six kids are in line for a conference, we need to take note of their concerns and think, "How can I help them rely on me less for these issues?" Perhaps the first two children who are waiting in line believe they are done with their stories and wonder what they should do next. It would be very easy to tell them to get new paper and to help them get started on a new story. But if we are teaching independence, if we want kids to make their own decisions and to proceed with self-reliance through the writing process, then we need instead to help them know they can solve their own problems: "There's not one writing teacher in this class but twenty-six of you. Every one of you can be a writing teacher and help your friends make decisions about writing." Unless we release ourselves from the job of being micromanagers, we will not be free to move among kids, to observe them at work, or to intervene to lift the level of today and tomorrow's work.

We can also predict the kinds of materials we may need in our conferences, though they will vary according to the unit we are teaching and the particular focus of our conferences within that unit. Many teachers have the following items with them as they confer:

- Record-keeping system
- Blank pieces of paper and blank, premade booklets
- A writing folder with pieces of writing (yours and student exemplars)
- A piece of literature (mentor text you have been using in the unit of study)
- Wipe-off board and marker, or pad and pen

Anticipate That Unpredicted Problems Will Also Occur and Invent Long-Term Solutions

We also need to know there will be unpredicted problems in our workshops, and we need to plan our teaching to allot time for studying and responding to them. The temptation when teaching writing is to keep ourselves so busy solving everything that we never get a chance to study the patterns in the problems and to look for deeper solutions.

For example, if the classroom feels loud during the writing workshop, it is easy to run around shushing people and never step back and think, "What underlying issues are creating this noise?"

Many teachers find it helps to schedule times for observing in their own classroom. Tell your students, "At the start of the writing workshop today, I am going to be researching, not teaching, so if you run into problems, help yourself rather than coming to me." Then force yourself to look and look again. Try to see the things you do not want to see. Then refrain from solving whatever dismays you. Let it go for now, while you try to think in smart ways about the ecosystem of your classroom. Pay special attention to patterns. Who is making the noise and what do those students have in common? When in the workshop do things seem to unravel? What might be the cause? Recruit students to help you understand. "I have noticed that this table seems to have trouble getting started on writing. What do you think is getting in your way?"

Sometimes, you will find that as long as you spend every minute managing the class, things proceed smoothly, and trouble only really starts when you hunker down to work with one individual or another for five-minute stretches at a time. Be wary of a relatively smooth writing workshop that is structured in such a way that you can't have high-level conferences.

Develop Management Systems That Support Conferring

In order to develop the management structures that support conferring, it helps to:

- Plan the logistics of conferences and teach these to children.

- Create an efficient record-keeping system.

- Be ready to alter your conferring style based on your assessment of your class' needs.

Plan and Teach the Logistics of Conferences

Most of the teachers I know confer by moving among tables of children, dragging a small chair. We pull close to one child in one section of the room, then criss-cross the room to hold a second conference in an entirely different quadrant of the room. I do not like to have children who want conferences put their names on a list because I want to be free to intervene where I decide to do so, and because I don't want children sitting passively, waiting for me to resolve their writing issues.

If the class seems restless, and I want my conferences to make an impact not just on one child but on a group of children, I am apt to say to the other children at the table, "Please put your pens down and listen while I confer with Joline." If there are children standing close to me, waiting for their time with me, I draw them in similarly. "Come listen," I say, pulling them in a close circle around the writer. I don't actually communicate with the eavesdropping children until the conference is over. Then I am apt to scan all the listeners and say something like, "So I'm wondering whether my suggestions to Joline gave any of you an idea for what you could do next as a writer?"

If there are children who feel they need my help while I am moving around the room conferring, I ask them to follow me as I work. I do not want these kids to stay at their seats, hands raised, until I get around to helping them. I find if they have decided they can't go farther without help, they often feel entitled to be disruptive if they remain in their seats. Of course, it inevitably happens that I soon have a tail of kids winding behind me. I'm prepared for this occasion. "Writers, eyes on me," I say, calling for the class' attention. "Look at what's behind me!" Then I tell kids that I need them to realize there is not one writing teacher in this room, but twenty-six. "You all need to become writing teachers," I tell them. This serves as my introduction to a talk, either on how they can help each other in peer conferences or on how they can help themselves (in which case we often make a chart, What Writers Do When We're Stuck).

Early in the year, children inevitably interrupt my conferences. Sometimes they have fairly important reasons; often they don't. Either way, I am prepared for the interruption, and ready to respond in a way I hope is instructive. "Mark," I'll say. "I was *conferring!*" I say this as if it is almost inconceivable to me that a child would interrupt something as precious as a writing conference. "Is it a matter of life and death? Do you need to go to the nurse?"

When I finish the conference, I will, of course, turn my attention to the children who are waiting for me, but even now, I want kids to realize that I value self-sufficiency. If one asks if she can get some more paper, my response will be, "What do you think my answer will be?" When she supplies the correct response, I add, "Next time, I bet you could figure that out all by yourself." My response to the next child might be similar. "Sarah," I might say, "I'm wondering if right now, you could solve your own problem. That's what writers do. We run into trouble, and we figure out a solution."

If I can keep children from running to me for every little thing, I can initiate conferences based on my own assessments of children and my hopes for the day and the week. I take a lot of different things into account in prioritizing conferences.

First, I use these interactions to keep as many children working productively as possible. There is no denying that the child who can't seem to sustain himself or herself ends up being something of a magnet for my attention. But I try to wean high-maintenance children from relying on me so much, and especially from relying on me to provide similar support every day. That is, if earlier this week, I helped two or three kids generate ideas for their writing, I do not want to provide that same help today. Yet some kids come to expect just this. My solution is this. If I have recently conferred with a child to help that youngster do something (such as generate ideas for writing), then the next time the child seems to need this support, I try to gather a small group of writers who want this assistance and I give it to them in a strategy lesson (which is essentially a small-group minilesson). This means that my help is less intense and personal. In this way, I withdraw the scaffold gradually.

Then, too, when prioritizing conferences, I am apt to confer in ways that support the unit of study. Early in a unit, for example, I try to get the classroom humming with the new work on which we are embarking. If this is a unit on revision, I confer to support revision; I use the resulting examples of good work to rally energy for revision.

Early on in a unit of study, I also try to assist some struggling writers right away so they get off to a strong start with the new work, and so I can showcase their efforts as exemplary. I know they profit from early opportunities to succeed, and that timely help from me can give them a foundation on which to build.

Once the unit is well under way, my conferences tend to be less aligned with the minilesson and the unit. Now what informs my conferences tends to be my sense of the pathways particular children need to follow as writers. If some children, for example, write word by word, inching their way through a sentence, I might decide it is time to help these youngsters write in sentences of thought instead of phrases of thought. For two days in a row, then, I might work with a small group of writers who could benefit from this practice. Then I might decide that another group of writers is ready to think not only about *what* they want to say, but also about *how* to say it well. Again, I might gather a few of these kids together and work with them across a few days.

Balance One-to-One Conferring with Small-Group Work and with Conference Fragments

It is crucial for teachers to spend some time each day working with informal groupings of children. If four or five children have a hard time choosing topics, focusing their narratives, or using the word wall, instead of giving each child a variation of the same conference, the teacher needs to gather these children for a group conference. "I pulled you guys together because it seems like you need help," the teacher might say. "Watch how I work with Donald." The teacher can then hold a public conference and end by saying, "Could the rest of you try to do what Donald just did? Do it while you are sitting here. . . ." Sometimes the teacher says, "Work on this for five minutes while I check the other kids."

It is also important for teachers to realize that sometimes kids need us to move quickly among them. It's not always possible to hold long, complicated conferences, and in those instances I recommend using fragments of conferences. For example, if the teacher is huddling in a corner with one child, carefully working though all the components of a perfect writing conference, but meanwhile the rest of the classroom is in chaos, the teacher might, instead, circulate the room, naming what children are doing that is working well. At one table she can say, "I've been watching you guys for a minute and I want to tell you the really brilliant work I've seen you doing. I saw a couple of you look at your picture and I could tell you were thinking,

"What should I write?" Then you wrote a sentence, like Davy wrote, "I rode my bike." But here is the really smart thing I saw. Listen to this. When Davy was done writing his sentence—and some of the rest of you did the exact same thing—he looked back at his picture again! He didn't just say 'I'm done' and jump out of his seat. No sir-ree! Instead, he did what real writers do. He looked back at his picture and I could tell he was thinking, 'What *else* could I say?' And look, he wrote another sentence. I bet he might even do this *another* time. That is such smart work. I am *wondering if* and *hoping* some of the rest of you might do the very same thing."

In this instance, the teacher simply gave a compliment (with perhaps a bit of a link). In another instance, she could simply teach, or do just the guided practice part of teaching. For example, perhaps she watched a child reread his paper without one-to-one matching. She might simply coach the child to point under words. "Can you read it with your finger?" she might ask. "Did that match? Did that come out even?"

The idea that sometimes we confer with groups of children and sometimes we use only fragments of a conference has been helpful to me and my colleagues because this means that when we need to cut corners, we can do so in principled ways. If we stay principled as we plan for independence, anticipate problems, and build teaching structures to support conferring, we will be on our way to managing the writing workshop efficiently and productively.

CHAPTER 3

❦

Efficient Record-Keeping Systems

The mere mention of record keeping makes most of us feel guilty.

We already know a dozen kinds of records we aren't keeping and a dozen more we should be keeping. Maybe we begin the school year with a new record-keeping notebook, neatly cordoned into sections, one for each child's progress in writing throughout the year. Maybe we carry a clipboard and portable record-keeping forms with us as we confer during the writing workshop. "I'm writing about my mom," one child says, and we diligently record the subject of that child's writing. "I'm done," the child adds, and we record that bit of information as well.

But then comes the trouble. Even as we are scrawling, "Brian writing about Mom. Done." we wonder what good these notes will do anyone, and have an anxious feeling about the answer. Or, we forget to transfer our carefully completed daily record sheets into the binder where they are meant to accumulate, and soon they're lost in a sea of papers. Perhaps we misplace the clipboard with the forms from last week, or forget to carry the clipboard with us as we confer.

Before long it's November, and our records are often so scanty that they make it appear we've conferred with almost no one and taught almost nothing at all. In dismay, we think "I can't salvage this now. I'll get a fresh start next year, and I'll be much more diligent!" and throw the misleading stack of forms away, leaving ourselves empty-handed.

Admitting this happens year after year is not a way of excusing it. We need to create a new ending to the story of our record keeping. This process often takes several steps.

Welcome Trouble

My first suggestion is this: We need to recognize signs of trouble, and stop feeling paralyzed by guilt when we find them. It is inevitable that when we set out on a mission, a journey, we will encounter trouble. In stories, characters always set out on a journey and encounter difficulty. The presence of difficulty doesn't mean that the journey (or the plot) is doomed; on the contrary, when the character faces a challenge, the story often grows more interesting, as does the character.

I find that I'm drawn to trouble the way others are attracted to a campfire. "Ah, yes!" I say with pleasure, pinpointing a source of difficulty. "This seems to be a problem for many of us!" I like finding that the problem is bigger, more complicated, more worthy than I first realized, and so I often search for far-reaching ramifications of the problem; I dig for deeper issues and implications. "Yup," I say with glee, "This is *definitely* a big problem!"

Peter Elbow, author of *Writing with Power*, once said, "The mark of a person who can sit down at 9:00 A.M. with one set of ideas and stand up at 11:00 A.M. with another set of ideas is a willingness to lift up the rug and to deal with all the troublesome loose ends—the tangles and problems that have been swept there." I couldn't agree more. I seek problems. Engaging in the process of unpacking trouble, of naming and understanding it, of developing new ways of working because of it, is one of the ways that my colleagues and I ensure that we continue to learn. Once I've spotted a worthy problem, I'm guaranteed a challenging and thought-provoking course of study.

This chapter, then, begins with the recognition that keeping track of our assessment is a problem for many teachers of writing. When we lift up our rugs, most of us will uncover the troublesome issue of record keeping. This problem need not make any of us feel guilty, however, as long as we do something about it once we've seen it. A problem like this one can be an invitation to make our teaching more effective.

Expand the Trouble

Before we go forward, we need to make this problem, like any problem worthy of study, bigger. If we expect that the answer will change our thinking from the foundations, we allow ourselves to look for answers in that wider realm. What are the grander, underlying issues? Dig deeper. We lose the record forms . . . why? We forget to carry them with us . . . why? It's not simply because we are thinking about buying holiday gifts or because our students are so demanding this time of year. It isn't that the form needs copying too often or that the shelf for the binder is too high. It's a big problem, not a little one. We don't lose our cell phones or forget to carry *them* with us. We don't lose our car keys or our lunches (well, not all that often). Why is it, truly, that we forget or let go of our record-keeping systems?

I think we forget to keep records of our conferences because so often we don't find them useful. We haven't figured out how the records can fit into the big picture of our teaching. If our notes aren't useful to us, why take them? Are we doing it simply because we are told to? If this is the case, then the record keeping is merely a tedious recording of what has passed, a hoop to jump through at the crack of someone else's whip. And then it's no surprise that in the flurry of all our urgent work, we end up forgetting to maintain them.

Check for Cover-Ups

If teachers aren't sure what to write down or why they're writing it down, and if they don't use the writing for planning, and yet they continue to keep records, I worry. Are we hiding behind record keeping? Does writing during a conference give us the illusion of productivity even when we aren't sure if we've taught anything worth recording? The teacher who records what Brian is writing about and records that he believes his writing is finished might even record the absence of something or other on Brian's paper . . . and then she might thank Brian and, without having taught him anything at all, move on, feeling pleased with having accomplished so much—after all, look at all her notes!

I think the first thing to say about record keeping is this: It is crucial that we don't deflect our attention from the issue of how to keep powerful records by engaging in useless, time-consuming note taking. If we do not have a pressing reason to record a note, we shouldn't write it. Records that pull a sampling of words from a conversation and plop them on a form someone has asked us to fill in can actually displace more meaningful interactions and more significant information collection. It is better to say to ourselves and those who ask for our records, "I'm studying record keeping in order to build a system that helps my teaching, so I'm temporarily between systems" rather than to appease our conscience and our supervisors with records that serve only to sap our energy.

Build a Solution

Record keeping matters because when we choose the form we will carry with us as we teach, we are deliberately channeling the mindwork that will surround the split-second, on-our-toes thinking that we do as we move among children. The best way to influence what we attend to as we circulate is to create (and zealously stay committed to) a form that requires us to record whatever it is we want ourselves to notice and to think about as we listen to and watch kids.

To illustrate what I mean, let's take a wild example. Imagine that I decided that during my writing conferences, I wanted my teaching decisions to be influenced by the color of my students' shirts—something I had never before considered as an influence. Cognizant that in the hurry of teaching, I usually don't notice shirt color in the slightest, I can make myself attend to the color of my students' shirts if I create a conferring form that requires me to record the child's name and shirt color. The form might even give me alternatives for what I could subsequently teach depending on the child's shirt color. For example, after recording that the child's shirt is blue, a fact I usually wouldn't notice, the form could ask me to check off which of three subsequent lessons for children with blue shirts I will teach.

Of course, that is a far-fetched example. But it is very important to realize that record keeping matters because the written forms we carry with us can channel our teaching. This means that deliberately fashioned record-keeping systems can focus the intelligence that surrounds our teaching. Instead of a form that pulls our thinking to our students' shirt colors, we can use a form to direct our thinking to the effect children's literature is having on our students' writing. The form would require us to record what influences from literature are evidenced in the child's pieces, and could list steps we could help children take to make that influence more fruitful. Alternatively, the form could ask us to note what strategies the child has used with independence.

Our records need to embody our teaching priorities. This means that if a group of teachers—perhaps all the second-grade teachers across a school—plan a unit of study together, they may want to translate their goals into a record-keeping form. For example, if a group of teachers decide that in September of the school year it is of primary importance that their children develop the strategies necessary to generate ideas for writing and that they are able to finish one piece and begin the next piece independently, then those teachers would want to create a record-keeping form for September that requires them to look for and record how well children are doing these things.

Using a Record-Keeping Form from Units of Study for Primary Writing

In the classrooms I know best, teachers either adapt the record-keeping forms that my colleagues and I devised for Units of Study for Primary Writing, or they develop their own version of these. Each unit in the series has an Assessment Rubric and an Assessment Checklist. Here we show the Assessment Checklist from the first unit, *Launching the Writing Workshop*. For the other checklists and rubrics specific to each unit, see those unit books.

You'll notice that on this form, the teacher lists all the goals and priorities for the unit. It is important that the goals are written in very specific and observable terms. For example, instead of including an item such as, "The child will be able to write with independence," a

Assessment Checklist for *Launching the Writing Workshop*

T - taught
O - must teach soon
/ - saw evidence that writer can do
X - saw more evidence that writer can do

Names

Goals												
Attitude Writer generates topics without resistance.												
Writer assumes the identity of "I'm an author!"												
Planning Writer chooses paper that is appropriate.												
Writer makes the transition from the minilesson to writing.												
Independence Writer cycles through the process with independence, starting a new piece when the last is done.												
Genre Writer's text conveys either a story or information.												
Purpose Writer knows writing conveys meaning. He creates coherent oral (or written) text to accompany pictures.												
Productivity Writer is socialized into the norms and mores of a writing workshop, carrying on productively for 20–30 minutes.												
Writer's marks show growing concepts of print (top to bottom, alphabet letters, etc.).												
Writer writes labels, sentences, or stories using sound-letter correspondence, etc., to do so.												
Graphophonics Writer has strategies for spelling unfamiliar words (at least stretches out a word, then hears and records initial or dominant sound).												
Writer revises by adding details into pictures/text and by adding more pages to text.												
Writing Process Writer uses resources appropriately to help with spelling.												
Writer tries to make his marks on the page match his mental image.												
Qualities of Good Writing Writer talks about the value of details.												
Reading Writer identifies print and understands its function in different texts.												

This checklist can also be found on the CD-ROM Resources for Primary Writing.

teacher is better served by writing, "The child can go from finishing one piece of writing to initiating another piece without needing guidance." Across the top of the table, the teacher lists the names of all the children in the class. This means there is a tiny space at the intersection of each goal and each child's name. Here, the teacher uses a 0 to indicate that this child might profit from instruction on this matter, a T to record that she has delivered some teaching on this point, and a slash (half an X) or a completed X to indicate that the teacher sees evidence of the child using this strategy with independence.

A record-keeping form like this one helps us in many ways.

- **Planning for conferring.** The form invites us to plan for our conferences, imagining—and in this way rehearsing—possible teaching points. This is important because too often, we approach a unit of study by planning for minilessons only. Some of our most powerful teaching will happen in conferences and small-group strategy lessons, and it is helpful for us to be required to work together in order to list possible teaching points on a shared Conference Record Sheet.

- **Observing strengths.** The form nudges us to observe children with an eye toward what it is the child can do. Because the form asks us to cross off what we see the child doing on his or her own, we are not stuck thinking only about the child's deficits. As we notice and record what the child has done well independently, we may well turn this observation into the compliment part of our conference.

- **Noting teaching options.** The form reminds us to think about and to record the many lessons that a child could learn from, even when we can't address many of them in the conference. The circles in the columns are a reminder for next time. Also, when we see that many children in the class have circles in a particular area, we can respond to their need with a minilesson or small-group strategy lesson rather than with conferences.

- **Widening our repertoire.** The form helps us remember that our conferences don't always reinforce today's minilesson. Instead, conferences are meant to remind children to draw from the cumulative list of all the lessons we've taught. The form itself lists the lessons from an entire month; it serves to remind us to help children draw upon a very big repertoire of skills and strategies.

Because we have a list of possible teaching points before us as we confer, we're less apt to restrict conferences to only helping kids put today's minilesson into practice.

- **Following up our teaching.** The form helps us to remember that any one day's interactions with an individual need to grow from and extend previous interactions. For example, we may notice that a child could benefit from learning to use quotation marks, and we indicate this with a circle. The next day, we might teach this in a conference and record this with a T. Another day, we notice the child using this independently in her writing, and we mark a slash (half of an X). In this way, the record-keeping form helps us plan teaching to build upon previous days' work.

Of course, it is not essential that every teacher adapt or create some version of this record-keeping sheet. But it is important to capitalize on the fact that record-keeping sheets are a way to channel the mindwork of our teaching.

Creating Your Own Record-Keeping Form

We might decide to create record-keeping forms that help us take on new priorities, different from those inherent in the design of the Units of Study form reprinted here. For example, if we resolved (for a time) to attend to whether our children have readers in mind when they write, then we could create a form that reminds us to ask each child, "Who will read your writing?" and, "What will you do with your writing when it is done?" Next, we would need to devise a plan for dealing with whatever children say in response. For example, we could develop a rubric for differentiating whether kids have a weak, medium, or strong audience awareness by laying out what each looks like, and we might watch and record how their audience awareness does (and does not) change in response to teaching strategies that are meant to support them in learning this facet of writing.

It is easiest to pay attention to some aspect of writing development—audience awareness or our children's use of literary language or their control of high-frequency words—if we are part of a study group that has convened around this issue. In fact, I'd go so far as to suggest that the question, "What will we record as we confer with our kids?" belongs at the center of any study group of teachers. The question is really a two-part one: "What are our goals as a study group of teachers?" and "How will we collect evidence of our children's progress toward those goals?" Then, too, we need to ask, "How can we, as a study group, set up a structure and a set of forms to help us collect what children show us in this area, so we can learn from it to become smarter as a group of teachers?"

Any form we carry will influence us. For example, if the form we choose is simply a grid of twenty-four (or thirty-six) boxes, each bearing the name of one of our students, then it can still coax us to cover more territory, to get to more kids, if only so that we can fill in more of the boxes. Once we embrace the direction of this particular form, we can maximize its guiding power by deliberately holding constant the length of time we allow ourselves to use one class-sized grid. If we give ourselves a new grid at the start of each week, then we'll be able to look back on any one completed grid to compare the total number of conferences we've held that week to the total number we've held in a different week. Are we improving in our reach from week to week? Once we have decided on the purpose of the form, we can maximize its use by thinking through the ways we fill in, compare, and file each one.

Study Your Past Work with Colleagues

Although I suggest we choose our priorities and then fashion those priorities into record-keeping forms, we can also design the forms from a different starting point. We can examine the record keeping we've already done, realizing that the notes we keep of children are also maps of where our attention has been. Looking at these records can be like watching our own thinking.

For example, if you have always carried with you a grid with a list of names down one axis and the date across the top axis, and if you have always just jotted something—anything—under each child's name, these records can reveal to you what it is you tend to notice (and not notice) about your writers.

It is easier to see what we have been doing—and not doing—when we look at the records of a whole study group of teachers, including people who have made very different choices. Otherwise, we may think, "I am recording the *only* things there are to record. How else could I write it, really?" If we look at each other's record-keeping sheets, we will notice that some teachers will have recorded the children's topics; others, the stage of the writing process in which each child was engaged. Another teacher will have recorded what he tried to teach—the teaching point—and what the child agreed to do subsequent to the conference.

What about you? Is it time to turn your attention somewhere new? Have you recorded what children don't do rather than what they are beginning to do? Have you focused a lot of attention on the child's level of productivity or the child's control of conventions . . . and might you deliberately want to try to alter your governing gaze so that your teaching takes into account new aspects of the child, writing development, and of your teaching?

CHAPTER 4

❦

The Research
Phase

Over the years, I've often asked teachers, "Over the course of your entire professional life, including all the staff development and workshops and summer institutes in which you've participated, can you identify moments that have been especially instructive, especially transformative for you as a teacher?"

Almost without fail, teachers respond by remembering times when someone has observed their teaching and talked with them about it, when someone has made them feel seen and understood. How desperately we, as professionals, need recognition. I do not mean we need trophies and awards. I mean we need someone who recognizes what we are doing and sees what we are trying to do. We also need someone who helps us to take a step forward.

Writers, like teachers, need to be understood. I will not forget when Susan Pliner, one of my writing teachers, read my draft and said to me, "In your rush to get it all down, Lucy, you sometimes jump too quickly from one good idea to the next as if you were greedy to tell it all—now. It's about patience." I knew she was talking not only about patience at the desk but also about patience at life. "If you can slow your eye down, your heart down, your mind down, you'll give yourself the opportunity to see what's really there," she added. That was twenty years ago, but I have held that sage advice close to me ever since. My goal when I confer is to be an equally astute researcher, and therefore to be so on-target that the child holds *my* advice close to his heart for decades!

Teachers who are learning to confer often say to me, "The hardest part of conferring is that I never know what to say, what to teach. I can do the research part of conferences, but then when it is time to teach, I feel empty-handed." I tell these teachers that they are right to recognize that the magic in conferring comes from knowing what to say, and that the answer to that question lies in the research phase of conferences. The knowledge lies in the teacher's interactions with a particular child.

During the research phase of a conference, we essentially ask, "How can I help?" The words in that phrase are easy to say: The question can roll off a person's lips as if it is a simple one. But it takes a lot of wisdom and finesse to look and listen and think with a young writer in ways that allow us, as teachers, to construct an answer to that question. During the research phase of a conference, we try to understand what the child is already doing and is trying to do as a writer, and what the child can almost but not quite do. We ask ourselves, "What might be the most important lesson for this child on this day?"

Of course, it is crucial to recognize that the research phase in a conference will always be inadequate. If you look over the conference transcripts, the research phase never lasts for more than a third of the entire conference. This means the research can't last longer than two minutes—at the most! In a two-minute intervention, we can't be *confident* that we have gleaned the child's intentions and ascertained the appropriate next steps for this child. But we can gather our wits about us and make our best possible effort to take cues from the learner . . . and we can proceed with humility into the teaching component of a conference, knowing that we may have misread the learner.

Component Activities

The research phase of a conference often includes these activities:

- Recalling what we already know about the child as a writer
- Glancing at (and quickly reading) what the child has been writing
- Observing the child at work without interrupting
- Asking questions and probing to explore the child's answers

Recalling What We Already Know About the Child as a Writer

Many of the conferences in this book (and on the companion CD-ROM, *Conferring with Primary Writers*) were conducted and written by me, Amanda Hartman, Zoë Ryder White, or by other staff developers from the Teachers College Reading and Writing Project. We are teacher-educators and do not spend all day, every day working with young writers, as do classroom teachers. The conferences would be different if teachers who work alongside these particular children all year conducted them. For this reason, in the conference transcripts, you see less evidence of a teacher recalling what she already knows about a child than you might expect. Still, you will notice that when I approach a particular child, Talia, for example, I recall that she often comes to school excited to tell stories about her weekends, her sisters, and her cats but that her writing doesn't tend to reflect the rich detail of her spoken stories. You will notice that when Liam is staring off into space, I remind myself that for this particular child, staring into space doesn't necessarily mean he isn't being productive. Ideally, as we approach a child, we also glance at our conference record sheet, using it to remind ourselves of what we have complimented and taught the child in previous conferences.

Glancing at a Child's Writing

When a child writes, the child puts his or her ideas and ambitions and knowledge base onto the page in such a way that we, as teachers, are given a window onto what the child can do independently. Even before we formally begin a conference, then, we often glance at and quickly read what the child is writing. Later, once we have spoken with the child, we usually look again at the child's work, this time letting the child's comments govern our lens.

The first question I try to ask when I look at a young child's writing is, What does this child seem to be trying to do right now as a writer?

My teaching is best when I teach into a learner's intentions (or help the learner form new intentions). For this reason, I generally begin a conference by asking the writer, "What are you working on as a writer?" I teach students that we want to know not only the nature of their project ("I'm trying to write a story about when I lost my shoe"), but also what they are trying to accomplish as a writer ("and I am trying to make it funny, but I don't know how to make it funny"). Older students become skilled at articulating their intentions, but, especially at the start of the year, very young writers need our help to do this. Often, I can glean a child's intentions from looking at his or her writing, and then I try to name these for the child. "It looks like you've been trying to write a lot of details about the football, is that right?" In order to articulate a child's intentions for that child, I need to ascertain them based on the child's work.

It is important to realize, however, that a child might be *doing* one thing as a writer while *working on* something different. For example, I recently showed a group of teachers Sudhir's draft (see Sudhir's Story on the following pages) and asked them, "What do you suspect Sudhir is trying to do when he works on this story?"

It was Thursday Morning
Suddenly I woke up "It's my belt test!"
I shouted very loudly as I jumped on my bed.

Then my mom came in my room.
She asked me, "What's so exciting?"
"My belt test. My belt test!"

And my mom calmed me down.
I dressed up in my clothes.
After that I ate breakfast and I went to class.

I ran right in class so quickly.
I told almost everyone that it is my belt test.
I was so proud of myself.
I was going to get my high yellow belt in ti-kwan-do.

Name: _____ Date: _____

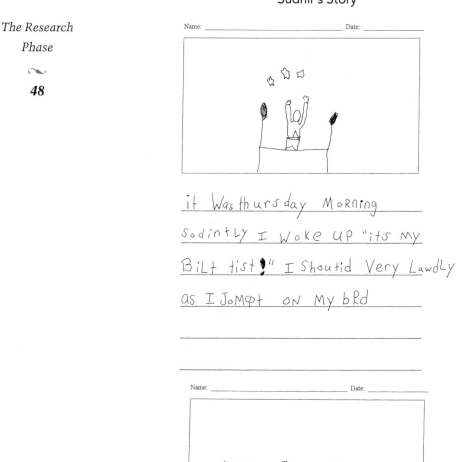

it Was thursday MoRNing
SodintLy I Woke UP "it's my
BiLt tist!" I Shoutid Very LawdLy
as I JoMφt oN My bRd

Name: _____ Date: _____

then
My MoM CaMe in My Room
She asct Me Wats so exiting?
My BiLt tist My BiLt tist!

Name: _____ Date: _____

and My MoM Comt
Me dawn· I Dristup in∗m y
Cloths· aftir that
I ate BRecfist and I Went
to CLass

Name: _____ Date: _____

I Ran Rite in Class So Qwecly
I told all Most ifRYone that it isMY
BiLttist· I Wasso pRoud of My siLF
IWas going to get My Hie ylloe BiLt
in tikWondo

Teachers who are familiar with Teachers College Reading and Writing Project terminology tend to respond that Sudhir seems to be trying to write a small-moment story—a story that pulls close around one instant. I agree that he is writing within that genre, but I think that writing small-moment stories is easy for him now, and his intentions are to *show* (rather than simply *tell*) that he was excited for his belt test. Sudhir may not be able to articulate this intention. If I'd asked him, "What are you working on as a writer?" he might well have responded, "I'm trying to tell about my belt test," but because of what I infer from the way he has written, I would add, "And it looks to me like you are trying to *show* that your belt test was exciting. You didn't just *say*, 'I was very excited,' did you? You *showed* it by saying 'I ran right into the class so quickly.'" I name what I believe Sudhir's intention might be to check my intuitions and to model the sort of talk about writing that I know he can soon learn to do.

In order to teach teachers how to "read" student writing, I might ask them to study another student's writing. On one student's page, they found blocks of color with color names accurately written below them. Between the color names were scattered letters; if these spelled a word, it wasn't decipherable. I asked teachers, "What do you suspect *this* writer was trying to do?" The teachers responded that the student, Gina, seemed to be writing a story about colors. It was true that she had written the names of four colors, but the scattered letters written below the lines, contrasted with the fact that she had spelled the color names almost completely and correctly, suggested to me that Gina had copied the color names from the classroom wall. My hunch was that she was not trying to write about colors so much as she was trying to make her page look like the other children's pages or like the pages in a book. She was so eager to put letters onto her page that instead of working to capture her own meaning, using whatever pictures and letters she could muster to convey her message, Gina had resorted to copying environmental print onto her paper.

Of course, as I study a child's work, speculating on what this child seems to be trying to do, I also ask, "Where in the developmental ladder does this child seem to fall? What next steps might be within reach for this writer?" After even just a split second of glancing at the work of these two writers, I have considerably narrowed my options for what I might teach.

Observing the Child at Work Without Interrupting

We try to watch a child for a fraction of a moment without interrupting in order to learn how he or she goes about working. If the child is writing, we notice how the child proceeds. Does he say a sentence aloud to himself and then write that whole sentence before pausing to reread it and to say aloud the next sentence? Or does the child say a sentence, then isolate and say the first word within that sentence, write that word, reread it, and then again say the sentence, continuing from there? Alternatively, does the child go from isolating a word to isolating a sound, shifting between writing and rereading several times within each word?

If you skim through the research components of the conferences in this book or use the CD-ROM, you will notice that especially at the start of the year, children are often not writing when we approach them to confer; instead, they tend to be drawing, getting a new piece of paper, rereading, or doing something else entirely. You might ask why no child seems to be writing at the start of these conferences, and I think the answer relates to the old saying, "Let sleeping dogs lie." In the fall, when a child is immersed in writing, we tend to leave her alone. It's hard to keep children writing, and we don't want to interrupt. We're more apt to confer with the child who is stymied; we pull our chairs alongside children who are in the midst of drawing, rereading, or the like.

When a child is drawing, we do not begin the conference by asking, "What are you *drawing?*" Instead, we treat the child's drawing as part of the writing process and ask, "What are you working on as a writer today?" We give careful, respectful attention to the child's drawings, and especially do this when the drawings are a big part of the meaning the child has represented. The questions we ask of a child's drawing vary depending on the genre we hope the child is tackling. At the start of the year, when we hope children are representing personal narratives on their paper, we often look at the picture and ask, "What's happening in the story?" "Are you in this picture?" and "What did you do next?" Later in the year, when children are writing information (or all-about) texts, we are more apt to say, "So tell me about this. I didn't know you knew about dump trucks. What are the important things your drawing can teach me?"

If we observe a child who does not seem to be working productively, we sometimes try the technique of pretending that the child *has* been doing exactly what we hoped he or she would do. We might, for example, draw close to a child who is making a magic marker tower and ask, "What are you working on as a writer?" Alternatively, we might address our concern directly.

Ask Questions and Probe to Explore the Child's Answers

When I first learned to confer, I carried a little sheet of paper with me to remind me of questions I could ask writers. You can make a similar scaffold if you study the conferences in this compendium and/or in the CD-ROM and collect questions you admire. These would be on my list of opening questions:

> Can you tell me what you are working on?
> What's your plan for writing time today?
> What are you working on in your writing today?
> How's it going with your writing today?

Such a list, however, is a bit misleading because the secret to effective questions lies not in the opening question, but in the way teachers respond to children's first answers with questions that probe and explore their responses. Notice, for example, in each of the following instances, the question listed above sets the stage for a sequence of extension questions:

> **Can you tell me what you are working on?**
> What happened first in your story?
> Are you in it?
> It looks like you drew some hearts and stars and balloons. Is there a story about them or are they just things that you like to draw?
> So did you just make pictures and not think of words that go with them?

> **What's your plan for writing time today?**
> I notice you haven't been using our precious writing time all that wisely. Have you noticed that about yourself too?

What are you working on in your writing today?

What do you mean you can't write without help? You were writing
   without help last week. What has changed?

Are there pieces in your folder you might like to go back to?

How's it going with your writing today?

I see you have a booklet of three pages in front of you. Are you
   planning to write a true story about something you did, and to
   have it go across pages?

In these sequences of questions, more than once I feign ignorance.
For example, when the child tells me he is trying to write about a feeling
"like Angela did," I have my own understanding of this. Yet still, I
say, "What do you mean [when you say you are trying to write about
a feeling like Angela Johnson did]?" I know very well how Angela
writes about feelings, but I want to understand *this writer's* understanding of the mentor text. In a similar way, I sometimes feign ignorance of code words like "revision" or "good leads" so that I can glean
what those terms mean to the writer. "So you said you are going to revise to *show don't tell,*" I'll say. "What do you mean by that? How do
you *show not tell?*"

Some of the follow-up questions rely on the teacher's knowledge
of what the writer is already doing. Journalists have a rule of thumb:
"You need information in order to learn information. The more you
know, the more you can learn." If I am not sure how to learn more
about what a child has said, I often name what seems evident to me
about the child's work. For example, if I saw a child who was obvi-
ously having trouble getting started on a poem, I *could* simply ask,
"Can you describe your writing process for this poem?" But I find I
learn more if I name what is evident: "I see you have five discarded
starts, all crumpled up beside you. It looks like you are having trouble
getting started on this poem. Can you tell me what you've been
thinking and what's giving you trouble?"

Predictable Problems That Emerge During Research

The research phase of a conference can present some predictable problems:

- The research phase sometimes lasts too long.
- The research sometimes doesn't influence your teaching.

These problems can be tackled in several ways.

The Research Phase Lasts Too Long

If you study our conferences and examine when the research phase ends and the teaching begins, you will notice that the research consumes about 25 to 30 percent of the conference. Look through these transcripts and those of your own conferences to notice patterns. You may find that you devote more like 75 percent of your time to research. If this is the case, you are not alone.

There are several possible explanations. First, in the name of research, you could be asking a lot of content questions about the *topic* of the child's writing. Notice the questions we do and do not tend to ask during the research phase of a conference:

Questions We Might Ask During Research Phase of a Conference	Questions We're Not Apt to Ask During Research Phase of a Conference
Rachael, what are you going to work on in your writing today? Can you tell me your plans for your story?	You are writing about when your mom left without kissing you goodbye. Where was she going? How did you feel when she left? What did you do?
Allison, what are you working on as a writer today?	Can you tell me how you felt when you were getting your ears pierced? What were you afraid of? Did your dad make you feel comforted?
Angela [a mentor author] did write about feeling scared. . . . Do you remember how she did this? So in your story, how will you do it?	What did you do next at the beach?

I am not saying there is no place in a conference to ask content questions such as "Where were you?" or "What did you do next?" or "How did you feel?" *but these questions are asked as part of the teacher's effort to improve the child's writing . . . not as part of an effort to understand the writer.* If these questions (and similar ones about the *topic* of the writing) belong in a conference, they should be part of the *teaching*, not the *research*. Furthermore, if we are going to ask questions such as these, it's really important to teach the child to *ask* as well as to *answer* such questions, or we run the risk of improving the child's text and not improving the child as a writer.

Notice, for example, in Natalie's conference with Justin, her questions during the research phase include, "What's your writing work today?" and "What are you thinking of doing next?" and "Which story do you want to tell? Is this the story of you and your mom getting stuck in traffic, or is it about getting shoes?"

Then, later in the conference, Natalie makes the decision to teach Justin to plan his narrative by anticipating what he will write on each page of his book. Now, in an effort to guide Justin to say his story aloud as he touches each page of the book, Natalie asks questions designed to lure Justin to talk about his topic. "Can you say more about that, Justin? What did you and your mom do while you were stuck? What happened next?"

When the research phase occupies more than 25 percent of a conference (or when the conference itself is more than five minutes long), the reason may be that the teacher was reluctant to make the transition from research to teaching. Perhaps the teacher could not figure out what to teach, and hoped that by prolonging the question-answer repartee, a bolt of insight would appear and a path open.

Activities for Making Your Research More Efficient

Teachers who find that they are often reluctant to take the plunge and decide on a direction for writing conferences may profit from the following activities.

- **Work with a partner who helps you to externalize the research phase of your conferences. Allow yourself only two minutes for questioning the writer, but give yourself time and companionship to think about what you learn.** After the two minutes are up, force yourself to stop interrogating the writer and to instead rely on *thinking* as a source of direction. For now, give yourself plenty of time for thinking after you stop questioning and before you begin teaching (at least while you are in training!). Try thinking aloud, exchanging conjectures with your partner. Ask yourself, "What might this writer be intending to do? What can the writer already do? What might the next steps be?" Do not expect a single convincing answer to pop out at you. You should find yourself entertaining a few possible hunches about the writer. Expect to muddle your way to some tentative theories about the writer. Out of those theories, you and your partner should be able to develop a tentative teaching plan.

- **Keep in mind that your goal is to learn enough to discern what the writer is trying to do, able to do, and not quite doing.** You may even want to have these questions (What is the writer doing? What is the writer trying to do? What is the writer not quite doing?) written down to carry with you as you confer. Keeping these three main points in mind as you confer will help you to focus your observations of the child's work and process.

- **Look at student writing with colleagues.** Working together, you can become proficient at looking at student writing, imagining what the writer seems to be trying to do, is able to do, and ready to do with a bit of support. Do the same for several writers. Use this preparatory conversation with colleagues as a backdrop for conferences. Confer with the writers after you've discussed their work. Before you meet with them, imagine: If this student were here, what three questions would you want to ask? This will help you develop more informed questions that could only be answered by the writer.

- **Skim through many of the conference transcripts, studying how other teachers make the transition from researching to complimenting.** You'll notice, for one thing, that sometimes this transition is a bit abrupt . . . and that is okay. Try to incorporate the same moves in your conferences.

- **Look over the transcripts of conferences in this book (and on the CD-ROM, if you have it) and notice that in about a third of the conferences, the instruction that the teacher gives to writers feels as if it was chosen fairly arbitrarily.** For example, the child thinks she is finished with her writing and revision. The teacher says, "Could I teach you one more thing . . ." and proceeds to take the writer toward any one of a great many equally valid directions.

You can do the same thing! Granted, at least half the time, your teaching decision should be rooted in recognition of what the writer has already done or is trying to do. But there will certainly be other times when a bit of quick research *doesn't* yield any one direction, and therefore you simply make a choice and move on.

Notice that if the teaching point feels arbitrarily chosen, the teacher tries to recruit the writer's enthusiasm for the new direction with a comment such as, "I've got one suggestion for something new you could try to do as a writer, if you are game for another challenge. Are you up for that?" (wait for consent) "Because writers often find that. . . ."

- **Study the conferences in this book and notice that there are very few instances when a teacher asks a question for which he already has an answer.** Sometimes when teachers are reluctant to make a transition from researching to teaching, the two phases of a conference blend together, with the teacher coyly weaving leading questions into the research so as to manipulate the writer into discovering and naming whatever it is the teacher hopes to teach. For instance: "And what do you think about your lead? Do you think it will really grab a reader's eye? How could you make it more interesting?" or "Do you think it is easier to read words when they are squished together like this [with no white space] or when there is white space? So what do you think you could do to help people read your writing?" These kinds of questions are problematic. Sometimes these patterns exist because teachers have been taught, above all else, to avoid "taking ownership away from the writer." Other times, the problem is that teachers have not been taught to ask questions that elicit information from students, but rather ask only questions that lead the student toward the teaching point the teacher already intends to make.

  Instead of asking known-answer questions, the teachers in these transcripts tend to ask authentic and honest questions. If the teacher has something to say (e.g., it is easier to read texts when the writer leaves white space between words), then the teacher is unabashed about coming out and saying whatever he or she wants to communicate. Reflect on transcripts of your conferences to see if you are asking known-answer questions. If so, you may be blending research and teaching.

The Research Doesn't Influence Your Teaching

For some teachers, the research phase almost never influences the teaching decision. In at least half and preferably two-thirds of our conferences, it should be clear that the direction of the conference emerges out of the research. That is, it should not feel like the teacher checks in with the child, and then teaches what he or she had in mind to teach in the first place . . . or that the teacher checks in, then arbitrarily pulls something out of the sky to teach. Having said this, let me also say that when teachers are learning to confer (and afterwards, too), they do both of these things fairly often!

In our conferences, there are many instances when we use the insights gleaned from our research to tailor a plan of action that is made to order for a particular child. In my conference with Annabelle, "Are You Doing Revision Work That Makes Important Changes?" for example, I notice and support the fact that she has revised by adding a hair bow into the picture and a few words into the text. Then I go on to say, "But revision is about making *big* changes that make your writing a *whole lot* better . . ." and I teach her to do just that. Similarly, Aziz, in the conference "Are *All* of Your Words Important to Your Story?" has revised by adding extraneous bits onto his Canada story; I point out that, although it is great he has added onto his text, revision often involves *taking away*, not just adding on, and I teach him how to do this. Then, too, Owen, in the conference "What Does the Rain Remind You Of?" explains that he is writing about rain and struggling to keep his poem from being boring. He isn't sure how to make a poem exciting . . . and I teach him that poets make poems special by trying to find new ways to describe things. In these and other such instances, we get direction from follow-up questions that show how well a child is achieving his or her goals. After Owen said he was working on a poem about the rain, I probed, "Oh yeah, I remember you started that piece yesterday. So what are you planning to work on with that poem today?" He responded, "I want to make it sound better. It just sounds like a boring story." Again I probed, "What are you saying about feeling like your poem is boring? Can you say more about that?"

However, this collection of conferences also contains many instances when research reveals only that the child is pursuing a productive direction, and it does not reveal any particularly necessary next steps. The teacher is left to conjure up a next step, relying mostly on the child's writing and on her previous knowledge of the child's abilities to inform the still almost arbitrary choice of next steps. For example, when I conferred with Rachael in "Are You Sure You Are Done Writing?" she had just finished taking a topic from her Tiny Topics notepad and written it as a little story. ("I thought my mom had left me. I looked for her and I couldn't find her. And I looked some more and then I found her.") She was looking forward to reading her story to the kids. My challenge in this instance was to imagine and launch Rachael on some further work, and the research phase of the conference had given me little to go on. All that I'd learned, really, was that Rachael produced stories quickly and easily enough that a lesson in rereading and revising seemed warranted . . . and the rest of my direction came from examining her piece, thinking, "What is something I could teach Rachael to help in a fundamental way with this piece as well as future pieces?"

Sometimes the research yields only one main conclusion: that the child is off track. The child may be playing or drawing or talking or copying or making up fictional stories or stalling; either way, the teacher aims to redirect the child toward writing true stories. In these instances, it is interesting to notice how the teacher goes about redirecting the child (in the teaching component).

Activities for Making Your Research Influence Your Teaching

Teachers who find that their teaching is often unrelated to their research may profit from the following activities.

- **Work on teaching your students how to have and name particular writing goals.** Across the year, conferences begin with the teacher asking, "What are you working on as a writer?" or a question that accomplishes the same purpose. Contrast the answers kids give in the first two units of study and in the last two. Notice that across time, kids become more proficient at having and naming particular writing goals, which in turn means our teaching can be informed by the writer's goals. Consider whether your students are becoming equally proficient at having and articulating writing goals. If your students aren't growing in their abilities to articulate what they are doing and trying to do as writers, study the conference with Marley, "What Is the Most Important Part of

Your Story?" to notice particular moves teachers can make to strengthen these skills.

- **Examine student writing to notice what the writer is already doing and to consider what steps he might take next.** While our conferences are always informed by what students have to *say* about their work, it can be useful to simply examine the writing on its own to practice noticing not only what students are doing well (which tells us what they know as writers) but also to discern potential "next steps" that the students could take. For example, if we were to examine a piece by Celine that shows a picture of her and her mom buying flowers (simply two stick figures and a swatch of red to represent flowers), we could see that she knows that writers can write about their own experience, that writers draw representationally, and that writers tell stories of something that *happened*. A potential and logical next step for Celine might be to include more detail in her pictures. You may decide that you want to study transcripts, in this book and/or on the CD-ROM, that illustrate the same teaching points you think a particular student of yours needs.

- **Examine the conferences in this book to notice how the teaching points are connected to the research.** It can be helpful to identify, after reading through the research components of the conferences in this book, what exactly the teacher has decided to teach. Look at the teaching point, and then look back at the research. What did she see or hear that led her to that particular point? How exactly did research inform the teaching point?

- **Practice conferring with a colleague.** It can be very helpful to confer in teams of two so that one person can be conferring while the other is observing, noticing what the child is working on and saying about what he is working on. Before making a teaching point, stop the conference for a moment and discuss with your colleague what each of you has noticed, and think together about how your new knowledge may influence your teaching point. Having two people's brains working together is an invaluable way to expand your horizons (different teaching points may pop out in the brains of different teachers). You also are more apt to hold yourself accountable for making your teaching match your research when you have a colleague to help!

- **Write a transcript of your conference.** Share and study it with a colleague or in a study group. You may want to find conferences in this book to compare and contrast. This will help you see the strengths and also raise questions about changes or ways to make either conference better.

CHAPTER 5

❧

The Decision Phase

The decision phase of a conference is the most mysterious phase of all because much of it happens "underground." One moment the teacher is researching a child and the next moment, she is teaching. The transition from researching to teaching happens in the teacher's mind, out of view.

My colleagues and I at the Reading and Writing Project spend much of our lives inside other teachers' classrooms, conferring in front of other teachers (or listening as other teachers confer in front of us) and then talking about the conferences. As I said earlier, the question teachers ask more than any other is this: "How did you know to teach that?" The interesting thing is that in teaching writing, we often unmask our own processes as *readers* and *writers*, thinking aloud in front of our kids so they learn how good readers and writers think about texts. We need to also unmask our processes as teachers. We need to say to colleagues, "As I research this child, I'm going to talk about what I'm noticing and planning so you can listen to my thoughts. You'll see me weighing possible ways to respond, and ultimately you'll see me make a teaching decision."

If you listened to me think aloud as I confer, you'd quickly see that I rarely feel certain that I've made a correct decision about the path a young writer should follow. Instead, I gather some clues and move toward a teaching decision with hesitation. That decision actually contains three separate parts:

- I decide what the child has done well that I want to compliment.

- I decide what it is I want to teach the child—something I hope will help the child with this piece and with future writing.

- I decide how I will go about teaching my teaching point.

When you are learning to get better at the decision phase of a conference, you need to allow yourself to slow down so that you have the time to push past your instant, initial ways of responding to student work. For this reason, you would benefit from looking at student work outside of class time and thinking about the decision you might make for this student. When you study the piece of writing, assume you had only the student's work to rely upon, not his history, and recall the questions I described earlier: "What does this student seem to be trying to do as a writer? What is succeeding? How might I especially help this student?" It will help if you recruit a colleague to join you in looking over your student's writing, and then have grand conversations about your different viewpoints. This can help you outgrow your own ways of seeing.

Another way to become more skilled at the decision phase is to confer with a teaching partner at your elbow. I suggest that the person who is functioning as the teacher in the conference be told that she can pause at any time to talk with her research colleague. You can talk right in front of the child—writers can benefit from eavesdropping on our reflections! Muse together about what you are noticing (remembering to notice what the child is able to do, is trying to do, and might need more help on). Often questions will arise that will require you to do a bit more research. Again, talk over your thoughts. Muse together over alternative ways of proceeding. The talking you and a teaching partner do together will resemble the thinking you want to do on your own another day.

Finally, you can use the transcripts in this book as a place to practice conferring. Read over the research phase of a conference, and then resist the urge to read on until you have first thought about (and ideally talked about) the decision you might make if you were in the teacher's shoes. Then compare the decision you would have made to the one we made. When you do this, keep in mind that ours is not "right" and yours "wrong." Any one conference can proceed in lots of possible directions. Some choices will be better than others, so you may want to ponder which choice would have worked best, and extrapolate some principles from the comparison.

Decide What the Child Has Done Well and Offer a Lasting Compliment

When you are making decisions in a conference, your first decision is this: "What has this writer done well that I can compliment and therefore reinforce?"

There are lots of reasons to begin with this question. First, we need to keep in mind that the child has just opened himself or herself to us. Everyone who has ever written knows the awful vulnerability we feel when we show our rough draft to a reader. "Writing is but a line," Mina Shaughnessey writes in *Errors and Expectations*, "that creeps across the page, exposing as it goes all that the writer does not know. The writer has put herself on the line and she doesn't want to be there." It is easy as a teacher to take hold of someone else's work and to look at it with eagle eyes, searching for flaws we can correct and errors we can fix. When we approach conferences knowing that our immediate response after the research phase of a conference will always be to give the child a long, meaty, powerful compliment, then we read the child's work thinking, "What can I gush over?" This transforms our body language, our mind-set—and above all, our relationship with the writer.

You may want to reread lots of our conference transcripts, looking only at the compliments, thinking, "What can I learn from these examples?" Here are a few of my favorite examples:

- "Shiwhan," I said, "You wrote two pages! Congratulations! When I look at your pictures and read your words, I can tell that you have so much to say about your trip to Korea. You've written just like authors in real books with a picture up here, and your words down here. You should do this always when you write!"

- "Justin, I am so glad you told me this because I had no idea about that traffic jam, *or* the shoes! Are those the shoes you got that day? They're nice and clean, aren't they! Lucky you." Then Natalie added, "Justin, you have done some smart work here. You told what happened first, and next, and you told it in tiny detail. On the traffic jam page, you explained how you sat there and sat there and then finally moved . . . and on the shoe store page, you told about the two pairs of shoes and the free shoes. Telling little details *in order* is really smart work. You really created a picture in your mind and put it into words." Then Natalie added, "A lot of things happened in that day, didn't they! I am the same as you. I would definitely want to write about a day that had so many adventures."

- "Two things please me about what you're doing. I love that you can show me the revisions you've made, Annabelle. It looks like you have thought to yourself, what else can I add to my drawing and my writing? *And* I love your energy for revision. I guess you are the kind of writer who is willing to work hard to make your best work even better! Annabelle, whenever you revise, always remember to ask yourself, What else can I add to my writing to make it better?"

- "Sasha, I love it that when I asked what you were working on as a writer, you not only told me your topic, you also told me what you are trying to do as a writer. You're trying to do something you've seen another author do! That's so professional of you! Always give me details like this; that way I know how to help you."

- "You were smart to ask Justin to be your writing teacher and to help you come up with ideas for your writing. I hope you continue to use your friends as writing helpers, Courtney. Good writers do that."

Ideally, compliments double as teaching points because they allow us to support something that the writer has just begun to do, or has gestured toward doing. So if a child has been writing small, focused narratives for weeks, including detail in them, and she has recently reread her story about a friend's birthday party and added, "The birthday party was at Chelsea piers," we *could* compliment the child for adding details. But we would be wiser to support the child for something more sophisticated, such as for developing the setting of the story. The techniques we use when we compliment a child's work are techniques we also use in minilessons, midworkshop interruptions, and teaching shares, because these are all occasions in which we point at good work (whether it has been done by a child, by us, or by an author does not matter) and try to help the child extrapolate some transferable lessons from whatever works. Here are some of these techniques.

- We often make children aware of what a writer *has* done by contrasting the positive example with a description of what the writer *could have* done that wouldn't have been as effective.

- We recall a specific and admirable thing the writer has done and describe the valued practice in such a way that this one specific becomes an example of a larger and more transferable quality or strategy.

- We praise and describe not only the product of the writer's efforts but also the process the writer probably used to create that product.

- We try to make sure that many of our compliments help the writer develop a sense of identity.

Compliment Technique: Contrast

Time and again we make children aware of what a writer *has* done by contrasting the positive example with a description of what the writer *could have* done that wouldn't have been as effective. Notice these examples:

> "Ford, I love the way *you didn't write 'all about' your Dad* but instead you *zoomed* in on one moment—when he read to you!"
> "What a grown-up, writerly answer, Oren! You are smart *to not just say, 'I am writing about when someone took my picture at the Halloween parade'* but to also tell me what it is that you are working on as a writer—telling me you are trying to slow down the important part!"
> "Owen, I love that great word you used, *streams*. It makes such a clear picture in my mind—*you didn't just say that the rain goes*

down the street, you used a word that shows *exactly* how the rain was going.

Compliment Technique: Generalize

You will notice we usually recall a specific and admirable thing the writer has done and describe the valued practice in such a way that it becomes an example of a larger and more transferable quality or strategy. In the preceding examples, for instance, I compliment Owen for using the word *streams* by letting him know that in this instance, he has done something transferable to other conferences. Specifically, he has *chosen a word that makes a clear picture and that conveys exactly how something happens.* Then I couch my support of a specific action by naming what is transferable about this action. When I compliment Oren for telling me that he has tried to slow down an important part of his story, I let him know that it is writerly to *tell me specifically what he was working on as a writer.*

Compliment Technique: Focus on Process

Often in a compliment, we praise not only the product of the writer's efforts but also the process the writer probably used to create that product, deducing it from the evidence. For example, after Oren told me that he wanted to elaborate on his narrative, I complimented him, saying, "What you are doing is exactly what writers do! *You chose a part that is important; you thought, 'Why is this important? What do I want my readers to know and feel here?' Now you want to slow that part of your writing down by adding on.* I hope you always do that. That's really smart." By praising the strategy the writer probably used, we give the writer support in using it another time.

Compliment Technique: Focus on Writing Identity

Many of our compliments help the writer develop a sense of identity. Many people suggest that when reprimanding a child, we scold the action, not the person. The opposite is surely true when complimenting a child. We make the compliments personal and word them in ways that help writers develop their own identity as writers.

One effective strategy for buoying a writer's identity is to tell the child he or she has written just like a professional writer often does. "Talia," I said in one conference, "It is interesting to me that you are going back to your cat and writing about her again. *Cynthia Rylant does the same thing! She writes a ton of stories about Henry and Mudge, and you write a ton of stories about your cat. You and Cynthia Rylant are alike."*

Compliment Technique: Combination

Any one compliment often combines many of these techniques. Let's study one as a case in point. Liam's story (shown on the following pages) involves a one-sentence caption on each page of a book:

> This is my garden.
> I like my living room.
> I like my bedroom.

Compliment	Compliment Technique
"Liam," Zoë said. "What a wonderful and interesting choice you have made in this piece—it looks like you have zoomed in on one topic, your country house, and then made each page tell about *one part* of your country house . . . this page is about your garden, this is the living room. Writers sometimes organize their pieces just like you did!	Zoë first notices a specific admirable thing Liam has done (he's written about one topic, with every page pertaining to his country house), and she describes the good thing in a way that is general enough to be transferable to another day and another topic. She illustrates the generalization with details when she points out that each page fits under the general topic.
Another cool thing about this piece is that you don't have other pages about school or your friend's house. Every page stays on the topic of your country house.	Then Zoë makes Liam aware of what he has done by contrasting it with the alternative, which he did not do. He did not include pages about school or his friend's house.
It reminds me of Angela Johnson's *Do Like Kyla*. She doesn't have other pages about her mother or her school . . . and your booklet is the same.	Then she tries to make sure her compliment develops Liam's identity as a writer by likening his book to a beloved book, *Do Like Kyla*. Again, she provides specific evidence for her claim that his book is like *Do Like Kyla*.

Decide *What* You Will Teach the Child

After you decide how to compliment the child, you will need to decide what to teach in this conference. You'll ask yourself, "What's the most important thing I can teach this writer right now?" Although we search for the "best" thing to teach a child, we need to remember that there is no one right answer. We take into account all that we know, but in the end there are many possible directions for a conference, and the choice is almost arbitrary. Still, there are principles we can follow in our teaching decisions.

- **Teach into the child's own intentions.** That is, if a student tells you that he or she is trying to do something (to add details, to write a good lead, etc.), try to find a way to teach toward *that goal* rather than taking the writer to yet another goal. If the child is trying to make a story more exciting, for example, you're more apt to equip the child to achieve this goal than to help the child write with more humor. You'll usually be able to imagine possible next steps for the child if you look at what the child has done so far, and examine specifically how the child has and has not achieved his or her own goals. For example, if the child is revising by adding details and has already added one detail—inserting one word (green) to describe the color of the dollar bill, you will want to think, "What has the child done in the way of adding details so far that I can celebrate?" and "What might the next step be in this child's journey toward becoming really skilled at adding details?" In this instance, I'd probably teach the child that surprising details are especially effective and show the child how I use observation to conjure up revealing and surprising details.

- **Teach toward independence.** This means that we will want to teach something we think the child is almost able to initiate on his or her own. For example, when Liam wrote, "This is my garden. / I like my bedroom. / I like my living room," Zoë *could* prop up Liam so that he *shows* how he feels about those rooms rather than merely *telling* his feelings with the phrase, "I like . . ." She could ask, "When you go into your living room, what exactly do you think about it?" and she could fish for phrases like, "I'm glad it's my house" or "I lie on the couch and think, this place is like a tree house." But the evidence she has from his work leads her to think that this is not something Liam could self-initiate another time on another piece. Therefore, she is more apt to teach him that after he has written one thing on a page, he simply needs to say more, to add another thing. That is, after writing "I like my living room," Zoë thinks Liam can learn to ask himself, "What else could I say about that and then add on?" Maybe this would lead him to write, "I like the big TV and the soft chairs."

- **Teach toward creating a community of writers who can support each other.** We are not apt to teach the same thing to every child. Instead, we help one child do one thing, another to do something different, and then we encourage kids to help each other and to emulate the admirable work their classmates do. Having said this, early on in a unit of study we tend to use conferences as a way to rally kids to the big work on the new unit. Once many writers are well-launched doing whatever it is that we are teaching in a unit, conferences are more apt to be tailored to the individual.

If you are not sure what to teach the child, you can always draw upon some ever-present options:

- Help the child use the strategy you taught in today's minilesson.

- Help the child think back over the strategies you have taught previously and incorporate one or more of them into his or her writing.

- Help the child progress to the next step of the writing process. If the child has just finished writing, teach the child to reread and revise. If the child has just finished revising, teach the child to edit. If the child has edited, teach the child to get started on a new piece.

- Help the child look over a mentor text by thinking, "What has this author done that I could perhaps try" and then help the child incorporate whatever she admires from someone else's writing into her own text.

- Help the child articulate what he could do to make this an even better text . . . then encourage the child to do just that.

- Help the child learn from (or teach) another child.

Decide *How* You Will Teach the Child

Before you proceed to teach a writer to do something in his or her writing, pause for just a minute to ask yourself, "*How* will I teach this?" You need to remember that telling is not teaching. Will you demonstrate? Coach the child to do this work while you are there to support? Explain and show an example? You should have a repertoire of teaching methods that you can call upon easily, and you need to remind yourself to plan your teaching methods even when you are teaching just one single learner. Don't allow yourself to ask, "What should I teach in this conference?" without also asking, "How shall I teach it?" Rely on teaching instead of on assigning.

In the next chapter, on teaching, I describe the teaching methods that are available to you when you confer.

CHAPTER 6

༄

The Teaching Point and the Link to Independent Work

When I was a young teacher, I lived during the school year in a summer beach house on Long Island Sound. One evening, as the sun sank over the sea, I leaned against a boulder on the edge of the beach and began to read *A Writer Teaches Writing*, by Pulitzer Prize–winning writer Don Murray. I remember looking up from the pages of that book and seeing the sun create a glittering path across the sea to where I sat, and thinking, "This book is giving me my path." It was one book that brought me into the field of teaching writing. I wrote to Don Murray, asked if I could meet him, and for two years after that, plunged into a course of study on professional writing. Every two months, I put my manuscripts into a folder on the car seat beside me and drove three and a half hours to the University of

New Hampshire for a twenty-minute conference with the great writer.

That was several decades ago, but I still remember what Murray taught me. Once I brought him an article titled, "Balance the Basics: Balance Reading and Writing." In the conference, Murray demonstrated how he often reads his drafts. He took my article and spread all the pages out in front of him as if they were a deck of cards, and then he looked between the pages to see the layout, the architecture, of the text. "For example, I'm noticing the disconnect between your title (Balance Reading and Writing) and the number of pages you've given to each subtopic," he said, pointing out that my division of attention didn't match my title. That was just one conference, one teaching point, but from that day on, I have read and taught with an eye toward the architecture of my texts (and my teaching). When I wrote this chapter, for example, it initially addressed only the teaching phase of a conference. The next chapter, addressing the link, was two pages long. By reading my draft as if the pages were the cards in a solitaire game, I saw the imbalance in chapter lengths and decided to include the link in this chapter. That is, decades after that conference with Donald Murray, I still use strategies that he taught me.

Ever since then, my goal when I confer with young writers has been to give those youngsters what Murray gave me. I want to teach them a strategy or give them a tool that they, too, can carry with them for the rest of their lives. I want to provide turning points in their lives as writers. The challenge is learning how to do this.

If we want to teach in ways that make a lasting difference, we need to care about what we teach, but also about *how* we teach. Murray's conferences may have made a lasting impression on me because he didn't simply tell me what I could do, he also *showed* me, and did so in a particularly effective way. Now, years later, I think my colleagues and I have begun to find the recipe to this magic. As we transcribed the nearly one hundred conferences and minilessons for this book, the CD, and the accompanying series, Units of Study for Primary Writing, we could see that our conferences and minilessons almost always draw upon one of a small handful of teaching methods. For this age level, these methods include:

- guided practice
- demonstration
- explaining and showing an example

Guided Practice

Guided practice is the most prevalent teaching method in our primary writing conferences. Nothing a teacher can do or say in a conference will inform a learner as much as the learner's own actions. When teaching very young writers, we usually have them try what we want them to do while we are still sitting alongside them. "Get started while I watch," we say, and soon we are scaffolding the child's work (providing guided practice) and then making a second compliment. In a conference that uses guided practice, after researching the writer, we suggest that the youngster try a particular strategy and then we set the child up to use that strategy while we coach into what the child does. In this way, guided practice allows us to give the child scaffolded experience using a strategy.

Think of guided practice as the method we use when we teach a child to ride a bike. "Climb on up," we say as we hold the handlebars and the bike seat. "I'm holding it steady." The child clambers onto the bike. "That's it. Now pedal," we say, and soon we are running alongside the bike. "Keep pedaling," we call, breathlessly, and then we let go for just a few seconds. "You are doing it on your own!" we say. Soon, however we've regained a hold on the bike seat. "Keep the handlebars steady. That's it . . ." Again, we let go. "You're off!"

In a similar fashion, we might use guided practice to teach a beginning writer to reread her work. "Sandra," we say, "can I tell you one thing writers do? Writers reread their work." We wait to see if she initiates doing this, and when she doesn't, we say, "Let's try it together. Put your finger under the first word." We wait, letting her respond to our directions. We adjust her finger so it is *under* rather than on top of the word. We wait to see if she begins to read her word aloud. If she doesn't, we say, "Read it, okay?" and when she starts reading, we are quiet . . . ready to scaffold if she needs help.

When we use guided practice, it is not enough to coyly maneuver the child so that she finds herself doing what we want her to do. Although we *could* have gotten the child to reread by simply beginning so she'd join us, we instead explain explicitly what it is we hope the writer will do. The teaching component of guided practice conferences in this book begins with the teacher naming the teaching point, just as we do in minilessons:

What I often do when I am trying to get ideas for my writing is I
 think of other authors who have done what I wish I had done. I
 am remembering that Julie Brinckloe had one of those "Ahhhh"
 endings. Let's look at it . . .
Lindsay, do you remember when we talked about revising by cutting and adding strips and taping our drafts? You can do the
 same thing with your how-to paper.
Isabella, I wonder if the story that you are planning might turn out
 [to be sparse] like Abby's when she wrote, "We heard the fire
 drill. We went out. We came in." 'Cause you don't have that
 many details either. . . . Writers need to tell details or readers
 can't get a clear picture in their minds of what happened. What I
 do to get details is I sort of act out what happened. Show me
 what happened first . . .

After explicitly telling the child what we hope he or she will
do, we help the child get started. Usually this involves bringing the
child to the start of the activity and setting her up so that she gets
started doing whatever it is we recommend. For example, after telling
Lindsay that writers revise by cutting and adding paper strips to their
drafts, the teacher tries to mobilize Lindsay to do this. "Show me the
part [of your how-to book] that is in the wrong place," the teacher
says. After Lindsay points to the spot, the teacher says, "So here are
some scissors. See if you can't solve the problem on your own—I bet
you can!"

In another instance, Amanda explicitly tells Lisa that writers
sometimes rethink their endings in hopes of getting one that makes
readers say, "Ahhhh." Then to mobilize Lisa, Amanda says, "Let's reread your ending and think about what works in it and what doesn't,"
and she and Lisa reread the last two pages of Lisa's book.

As the child proceeds to do the work, we support the child, usually with lean, efficient prompts. For example, once I get Annabelle to
reenact how she opened the present as a way of recalling the episode
and then elaborating on the draft, I intersperse prompts into her re-
enactment, so that over the course of a few minutes I scaffold her
work by saying:

Hmmm, I wonder what else you could add . . .
Show me how you picked it up. . . . Where did you write that? This
 information is so important. Where will you add that?

Keep going.
Act it out.
[a nod]
You think that will help people picture what happened?
You are a fast learner. Keep going.

It is not an accident that these prompts are precise, quick impera-
tives. When our teaching method is guided practice, we deliberately
avoid doing so much talking that we swamp the child's focus on her
work. Remember, our job in a coaching conference is to run alongside
the child as he or she rides a bike—or rereads, or adds details, or envi-
sions, or listens for the sounds in words—and to keep the child active
and successful.

Once the fledgling bike rider finds her balance and gains momen-
tum, we let go of the bike seat. We do this once briefly, then a second
time for longer. Similarly, once the child gets started doing what we
hope the child will do, we pull back, letting the intervals between our
comments grow longer. We still keep an eye on the child, and we're
ready to scaffold if that's necessary for the child to have a successful
experience. Of course, if we have just taught a child to do anything—
rereading his or her writing, reenacting an episode and then recording
exactly what happened—we need to expect that the child will only
approximate what we have taught. "That's it," we need to say, "Keep
going. You're catching on." We need to provide this support even
if the child's efforts are fraught with difficulty. When learners are
new at anything, their first efforts will be approximations and we, as
teachers, need to cheer their progress and support their willingness to
try something new. If we can lift the level of what the child is doing
with just a light touch, then we do so. But we can also accept work
that is less than ideal because it's the child's first efforts at something new.

Often when we support a child through guided practice, the child
works "in the air," not on the page. For example, we might help a
child recall what happened first, next, and after that in preparation for
drawing her story across three pages. Once the child has talked aloud,
we hope she will start putting the work onto the page. But before the
child can do this, we need to bring her back to the start of the spoken
version. At the end of guided practice, then, the teacher of writing often needs to take the child back to the beginning and set her up to do
whatever she has planned on the page.

Demonstration

When we are teaching writing, we are teaching people to *do* something. Whether we are teaching someone to swim or to play the oboe, to knit or to write, we are teaching an activity, and one of our most efficient, potent teaching methods is demonstration. "Watch how I put my face in the water and blow bubbles," the swim instructor says. "Watch again and this time notice that the water is up to my ear. Try putting your face into the water like I've done. That's it. Now watch how I turn my head so that my ear lies in the water, when I want to breathe. Now you try it."

As teachers of writing, we use demonstration in similar ways. First we name what we hope the child will learn to do; then we tailor a demonstration so as to highlight the one thing we really hope our student learns. Then we debrief, naming what we hope the learner saw. For example, in "But How Did You *Feel* in Your Story?" Amanda learns that Allison wants to emulate the author, Angela Johnson, by showing rather than summarizing how scared she was when she got her ears pierced. Amanda first articulates what she thinks Allison needs to do, speaking in ways that she hopes make a lot of sense to this six-year-old: "I think you need to build up the fear part by having it on many pages, so readers get scared and more scared." To help Allison picture what she has in mind, Amanda references a text they both know. "Remember when Joshua was scared and Angela [Johnson] had him walk past one thing, another, another . . . and only at the very end was he safe with his father? You need to bring your fear out over your pages too."

Then Amanda tells her young student how she goes about reaching this goal. "What I do is I remember what happened." Now Amanda begins her demonstration pretending to be the author of Allison's story: "I went in, I sat there with my dad, the guy comes, he says [whatever he said] . . ." Amanda is demonstrating how Allison could conceivably stretch out the fear part of her "Getting My Ears Pierced" story by stepping into Allison's place and pretending she, instead of Allison, is the author. Amanda needs guidance to do this so she checks in by asking, "What was the scary part of that story?" and then, after learning it was the needle, she tells Allison, "So zoom in on the part about the needle. Listen to how I might slow that down: 'I was sitting on my dad's lap, holding his hand tight. I saw the needle coming. I closed my eyes. . . .'" Then, having only demonstrated how to get started on this, she turns things over to Allison. "Now you try." To start Allison off, Amanda repeats her last line. "I closed my eyes . . ."

Allison picks up where her teacher left off. "The needle was coming. It was big and long. I squeezed my eyes tight . . ."

Later, Amanda will debrief for Allison, naming what she hopes Allison has learned that is transferable to other days and other pieces of writing. "When you are really trying to get your reader to feel something you are feeling, slowing down the moment so we can see it and feel it is a smart thing to do."

In this example, Amanda demonstrated for Allison using the student's own work and in this way got the child off to a running start using the new strategy. Amanda teaches in a similar way in the conference "Are You Stuck?" on our CD. In this conference, Amanda helps Sasha reread her writing, testing which line might become a good refrain. "Watch how I think about what might sound beautiful here," Amanda says and then rereads, trying first one and then another of Sasha's lines to see which would sound good if it were repeated as a refrain. Amanda deliberately tries out sentences that do not work, leaving space for the young author to step up to the plate and have success with this strategy.

Often teachers demonstrate using a text other than the one under consideration—either the teacher's own or one belonging to another child. For example, on our DVD, *Big Lessons from Small Writers*, Amanda confers with Harold, wanting him to tell a true story about something that happened in his life. In this conference, Amanda decides to use her own story to demonstrate to Harold what she means by "a true story that happened." So she says, "Pretend I was writing a true story that happened to Amanda." She pulls out a three-page booklet and points to the pages as she says, "One day I was swimming with my friend Mary." She turns the page and says, "We went splashing into the water." On the last page she points and says, "A big wave came and pushed us down under the water. I got water up my nose!" Then she says to Harold, "Go ahead . . . tell your story like that," and she coaches him to tell a true story about *his* life.

"What Else Could You Try That Mem Fox Does?" on the CD and in *The Conferring Handbook* (page 60) provides another example of a conference that relies upon demonstration. In this conference, I look with the child at *Koala Lou* by Mem Fox.

"May I watch how you go about studying what Mem Fox has
done? Can we look at the page together?"

The two of us read and reread the chosen page. I was silent, hoping Sudhir would comment on what he noticed, and he did.
"She tells that they waved their party hats."

"You are right. She doesn't just say, 'The spectators cheered,' she
tells *exactly how* they cheered. 'The spectators whistled *and
cheered and wildly waved their party hats.*'"

"Sudhir, let's name what Mem Fox did and see if she does that
again, okay?" I paused to see if Sudhir would step in and do this
but wasn't surprised when he didn't. "She used exact action
words, didn't she? Let's see if she does that on her page," I said,
turning to another page where she did do this.

Soon Sudhir had pointed to a section of the text that described Koala Lou's climbing. "Say more," I prompted.

"Well," Sudhir said, "It doesn't just say that Koala Lou climbed, it
says *how* she climbed. 'Higher and higher and faster and faster.'
She is going up that tree really fast," Sudhir said.

"Let's look at your piece, Sudhir. Maybe you could use exact action
words like Mem does to show *how* you do things? What are you
doing on this first page?"

"I'm shouting."

"Okay," I said, and lightly touched the page where Mem Fox's
spectators cheered by whistling and wildly waving their party
hats. I'm hoping to nudge Sudhir to use Mem Fox as a model.

"I can say, 'I shouted really loud'?"

"*How* are you shouting?"

"Jumping up and down."

"Put it together, Sudhir. Say what you'll write on this page."

"I was shouting very loudly, and I was jumping on the bed, too!"

I said nothing and watched to see if Sudhir would continue doing
more of this on his own. He continued, instead, to bask in his
success so I touched the next page of his book. "Come on . . .
keep going. There are other places where you can add *how* you
did things. I'll come check on you after you work for a while."

Teachers who want to become more skilled at using demonstrations as a teaching method within their conferences will want to
carry their own unfinished writing (a text that resembles what the

kids are working on) with them as they confer, and become accustomed to saying to writers, "So if I was going to do that on my draft, watch what I'd do." For example, a teacher could demonstrate how she rereads to decide on the important part of a story, then puts a box around that part and, taking new pages, says to herself, "I'm going to write about that again on this paper but this time, I am going to make a movie in my mind of what happened and tell it bit by bit, stretching it out." Alternatively, a teacher could use demonstration to show how she rereads her writing, checking to see if the words look correctly spelled, and how she takes any word that looks funny and tries it again, three different ways. In either example, after the tiny demonstration, the teacher would want to debrief, saying, "Did you notice how I. . . ?" Then the teacher would probably want to take the child to the place where she could start doing similar work, and launch her in that work.

Explaining and Giving an Example

When I think about the memorable conferences that I've received as a writer, as a teacher, or as an organizational leader, it is clear to me that some of the time, my teacher has studied my work—looking either at the process of my work or at the results of it—thought carefully about ways in which I could lift the level of what I'd been doing, and then explained to me what he or she believed I should do next or should do differently. The interesting thing about conferences that proceed in this fashion (research, assign/explain, give an example) is that this is how top-down supervision generally proceeds. That is, the format for this kind of teaching can be a recipe for powerful teaching—or for disaster. It is worthwhile, then, to try to differentiate between instances when this teaching method has been used more and less effectively.

The most important thing to remember is that the effectiveness of this teaching method can be evaluated based on whether it lifts the level of the learner's work today and in the future. If a teacher observes what a learner is doing, tells the learner that he or she should be doing something differently, and the learner either can't or won't translate the input into improved practices, then almost by definition, the teaching has not been successful. This is easy to say and sounds obvious—but if all of us, as teachers, really took responsibility for our students' successes and failures, this would utterly transform education. For now, schools are full of talk about what kids can't do. "He's a struggler, so he can't . . ." "She didn't learn a thing!" "No matter what I say, she keeps on . . ." "He's just not getting it . . ." What if it were really *our* responsibility to be sure he "got it"?

It is not easy to simply tell a young writer to do something and to have our words translate into new actions. Usually for this to happen, we must tailor the instruction so that it is very much within the learner's zone of proximal development. Then, too, we have to recruit the learner's motivations by making the new actions seem irresistible, significant, and worthwhile. Researcher and scholar of education Brian Cambourne points out that in order for us to learn from what someone else has done, that person's actions need to seem both doable and worth doing. From his window at the office, Brian can watch people hang gliding off a gigantic cliff. He sees them rope themselves up and then watches as they take off, running at a terrific clip toward the precipice, but because Brian definitely does not intend to follow in their footsteps, he watches with idle curiosity, and their actions do not enable him to do likewise. If a hang-gliding expert wanted Brian to learn from his example, that expert would first need to recruit Brian's motivation.

Natalie's work with Justin ("What Is the Most Important Part of Your Story?") provides a good example of this kind of teaching. Justin has already written a book in which one page tells about their car getting stuck in a flood, which caused a traffic jam, and the next page tells about arriving at the shoe store and getting two pairs of shoes. His plan is to add another page telling about having pizza with his cousins. Natalie says, "Wait a minute, hold on! I'm so confused. Which one is it? Is this the story of you and your mom getting stuck in traffic because of the flood, or is it getting shoes?"

So far, Natalie has researched and begun to assign/explain, but Justin is resistant. For her instructions to work, Natalie needs Justin's buy-in. So she tries another tack and suggests that Justin look at his story as a book full of various small-moment stories. She tells him he could write a whole book about one page, or about another page. Then, to help him imagine how this might go, she refers to an example. "Remember the other day, Serena's piece was just like yours—full of lots of different moments. Her book told about the swings and the bus and lunch at McDonald's. But remember how she decided to take just one page about McDonald's and just write about that?"

Often when we use this method, we refer either to our own writing or to published work in order to point out a particular thing that we hope a writer will do. For example, in "What Are You Teaching Your Readers?" Zoë wants to help Damien make the genre shift from retelling an episode toward teaching others how to do something. He has drawn an illustration. Zoë astutely zeros in on something that is very doable for Damien: "I think you need to work on making your pictures really help your words," she said, "Your drawings need to give us information that goes with the book. For example, let's look at the book I made, *How to Do Yoga.* See? I used diagrams to show specific poses and materials. If you want your picture to really be a good helper to your words, then you have to make sure that the picture you draw gives the information that you want to give."

Similarly, a conference I had with Carolina follows this same method. Here is an excerpt: "Carolina, it sounds to me like you are ready to revise like third graders do when they—like you—have so, so many ideas for how to make their pieces better. What they do is they get a whole 'nother piece of paper and they call this 'Draft 2.' Then they recopy the part of their first drafts that they like, changing whatever they want." Sliding a new paper in front of her, I said, "So label this Draft 2, like third graders do."

Tuck a Second (or Third) Teaching Point into a Conference

In an effective conference, the child leaves and is able to sustain a new level of work. Sometimes, however, we teach a child to do something and right there in the conference, the child begins and completes whatever we have taught. We could (and sometimes do) move into the link, summarizing what the child has already done, reminding the child that this is worth doing often in the future, and then ending the conference. Frequently, though, we decide to make our conference a double-decker one by introducing a second teaching point. In "Reread as You Write, Noticing White Spaces and Spelling," for example, I taught Nicole to reread, checking for white spaces, and she got the hang of this so quickly that I decided to make a second teaching point, showing her how to make small changes while rereading.

Then again, sometimes conferences become double-decker ones because we teach a child to do one thing, but the child quickly finds himself or herself combating a new challenge, one that requires a new teaching point. For example, in "What Is the Most Important Part of Your Story?" Amanda first helps Marley decide to write about just one thing—the end of her play date when her Dad arrives. But she doesn't want to leave Marley to do this without support, so Amanda shifts and begins to teach Marley that she can rehearse for narrative writing by touching the pages and saying her story aloud.

Linking the Conference to the Child's Ongoing Work

Writing conferences usually end with the teacher reiterating what she hopes the child has learned and reminding the child that this strategy is one that can become part of the child's ongoing repertoire, to be used often in the future. The end of the conference, then, is not unlike the end of a minilesson.

One of the challenges is that in order to name what the child has done in a way that is transferable, we need to back away from the specifics. In the conference "Let's Look at Your Lead and Your Ending," for example, Lisa studies *Fireflies* by Julie Brinckloe to get an idea for how to end her book, and learns that sometimes it helps to end a story with feelings. Amanda does not end the conference by saying, "You can always look at *Fireflies* for ideas" or even, "You can always end your stories with feelings." Instead she ends this conference by citing especially transferable things that Lisa has done. "You've done a lot of new things today that you are going to want to do again and again. Remember that you can always revise by checking your beginnings and endings, and that sometimes it helps to read what another author has done."

Sometimes, especially when conferring with young children, it is ambitious enough to simply reiterate what the child is doing and then give the child a little push to keep going. In "Can We Study What This Author Did and Let Her Teach Us Some Lessons?" with Liam, Zoë ends the conference by simply saying, "Liam, this is so cool. You are writing a many-moments piece, just like Angela [Johnson] did, but you made yours into a list of different rooms in your country house. Now on every page, you are adding in what you do in each of the places you write about. What page will you add to next?" (He answers.) "Great, keep going!"

Sometimes in the link, it is not the teacher but the child who restates the teaching point of the conference. "Which Part Goes Where?" ends with the teacher asking Lindsay, "Can you tell me what you just did?" The child responds, "I cut out the steps in my writing and put them in a new order!" The teacher affirms this, and then Lindsay adds on, "And then I read them. And now I'm gonna glue 'em back down." The conference ends with the teacher extrapolating from this conference a few strategies that are transferable to another day and another piece. "What a smart thing you have done! Always remember that writers keep scissors nearby, and if things are out of order, they cut and paste."

❧

CHAPTER 7

Supporting Reading Development Through Conferring in Writing

The writing workshop provides beginning readers with a powerful context for developing their *reading* as well as their *writing* skills. Actually, approximately half of the time that beginning readers invest in a piece of writing is spent on reading rather than writing. Many children reread multiple times as they write even a single word! And even when a child is involved in the writing part of composition, the skills the child works on in order to record his or her thoughts and stories are essentially the same skills that the child uses to read.

Writing is a perfect forum for teaching reading because when children write, they are active in a hands-on, concrete way. Then, too, when children are writing, they can (and must) attend to the micro-skills of reading and yet do so without losing hold of the larger

Supporting
Reading
Development
Through
Conferring in
Writing

∾

88

meaning of the text. If a child is writing or rereading about the muffin she had for breakfast, the child can belabor the middle consonant in the word *muffin* without forgetting its taste and story.

We can help students with reading during writing workshop even when they are at the earliest stages of emergent reading, using Elizabeth Sulzby's methods. Early in the year we help kindergarten children "reread" familiar books by looking at the pictures and retelling the story using "storybook language." This sense of story can be reinforced during writing workshop when we ask children to "reread" their own picture-based stories. We want children to understand that rereading means not only telling what happened in the story but also making it sound like a storybook. For example, instead of saying, "My story is about when I went to Six Flags," we want children to tell the story from inside of it: "One day I went to Six Flags," and so on. We can prompt students to do this as they reread.

Another reading strategy to focus on during both reading and writing workshops in kindergarten classrooms is using the pictures to help children understand the story. Because early writing depends on drawings to represent meaning, it can be important to highlight that drawings represent meaning in *all* picture books. This can work as a teaching point during reading workshop: "Just like in your story about your karate party, how you drew yourself in your karate outfit next to the cake," I told Danny, "the pictures here in *Along Comes Jake* help you understand what happened in Joy Cowley's story." In writing workshop, we can teach children to incorporate meaning into their pictures: "Take a look at *Caps for Sale*, Gina. Esphyr Slobodkina knew that her pictures needed to say what's happening in the story— look at the monkeys throwing down the caps. In *your* story, your pictures need to say what's happening as well."

When a beginning reader working with level A/B books rereads her writing, this provides the perfect context for helping that child develop the reading skills and strategies she needs to negotiate any text. That is, if a child is rereading her own story about the day she fell off the monkey bars but has trouble reading that she hurt her elbow (ELBO), the graphophonics work she does with letters on the page will occur within a meaningful context.

One way teachers can organize themselves to support their young writers' reading during the writing workshop is to bring the records they usually carry with them during reading time into the writing workshop, watching for and supporting the same strategies. Specifically, for example, the teachers with whom we work sometimes find it helpful to carry reading record sheets, such as the Prompts for Skills chart shown on the next page, during writing workshop.

You will notice that this reading chart lists the skills and strategies that we want to teach students at this level of reading. Underneath each skill is a series of prompts to give the students. The prompts range from providing the highest level of teacher support to the lowest level. This way, as you confer, you can observe the student and focus on areas in which the student needs support. As you refer to this chart, which you can keep at your fingertips, you can choose relevant prompts to support your student's particular reading needs. After you prompt the student, you then can then briefly record what you have complimented and what you have taught in the box containing the child's name.

You will also notice that this particular record-keeping form incorporates the names of all the children who are reading level A/B books. We refer to these children as Group 1 readers, although they do not sit together or see themselves as a group. (You can learn more about our ways of grouping readers and texts in *The Art of Teaching Reading* [Calkins].) If you are conferring with the children who are reading A/B books during reading or writing time, this chart allows you to scan the skills and strategies listed in the top section and note which of these skills and strategies this Group 1 reader is able to initiate independently as she reads or writes. It is important to especially notice, compliment, and record behaviors that the child is just beginning to demonstrate. It is not unusual for these breakthroughs to occur first in the child's writing and only later in the child's reading. By observing a child through this lens, you can become aware also of the skills and strategies that this Group 1 reader still needs (and that are in the child's zone of proximal development), and then teach one of those skills. You may do this teaching during the reading or the writing workshop. That is, we sometimes deliberately support the child's reading during writing time (and vice versa). This reading work can sometimes be tucked into a writing conference that actually focuses on writing goals, or it can influence what we ask children to do in the first place. Alternatively, during a writing conference we will sometimes teach toward the goal of equipping the child to become more skilled at rereading his or her draft.

Supporting
Reading
Development
Through
Conferring in
Writing

∾

90

Prompts for Skills

Prompts for skills, strategies, and habits to teach students who are reading Teachers College Group 1 level books

Prompts are listed from the highest level of teacher support to the lowest level of support.

Using one-to-one matching

- "Let me show you how I point under the words . . ."
- "Point under the words."
- "Does it match?"
- "Were there enough words?"

Using illustration as a source of information

- "Watch how I use the picture to help me figure out the word . . ."
- "Look at the picture to help you." (Teacher taps the picture.)
- "What could help you figure that out?"

Using cover (title, illustrations) to get ready to read

- "Watch how I read the title, look at the illustration, and think, 'What's this book about?'"
- "Check the cover."

Using and locating known words

- "Is there a word you know?"
- "What words do you know?"
- "Point at the words you know on this page."

Using meaning to figure out words

- "What would make sense here?"
- "What's going on here?"

Understanding the book

- "What's the whole book about?"
- "So what happened?"

Name:	Name:	Name:
Name:	Name:	Name:
Name:	Name:	Name:

Helping Group 1 (Level A/B) Readers During the Writing Workshop

The following strategies can help Group 1 readers improve both reading and writing skills during writing workshop.

Supporting One-to-One Matching

Children who are reading level A/B books are usually learning to point under words as they read and to do so in ways that suggest that they understand the concept that one spoken word is represented by one blob of letters. As readers, children learn to check that the words they "read" match (at least in number) the words on the page, and to self-correct if this is not the case. They learn that a three-syllable word is still just one word and that white space separates one word from the next.

Children can learn these foundational and complex concepts of print when they write. Certainly we will want to ask Group 1 writers to reread their writing, pointing crisply under each word as they read it. "Did that match?" we will ask in writing just as we ask in reading. "Did that come out even?" "Did you have any words left over?" It is important to ask these questions even if the child's oral text did match the written text because at this stage, we want to help kids ask themselves these questions (and to do so even when the answer is yes).

Although it is important for Group 1 writers to reread their writing to make sure that each word they utter is represented by a word on the page, because these children do not yet have control over the concept of word, they sometimes write strings of letters.

The easiest way to support one-to-one matching for writers who are reading level A/B books is to ask these children to write labels alongside the objects in their drawings. I encourage these children to label anything and everything—grass, sun, sky, whatever. The one-word labels not only provide plenty of white space around each word, they also demonstrate that one object may need a two-syllable label (e.g., rainbow). Then, too, the match of picture and label provides extra support to help beginning readers read these texts. Of course, children may use only initial consonants at first in their labels. Asking children to write labels means that they are not telling, writing, or reading the rich, storylike narratives that they could pretend to write (and could represent in scribbles or strings of letters). For this reason,

Supporting
Reading
Development
Through
Conferring in
Writing

∽

92

we might encourage children to label their drawings and then to storytell their stories as they turn the pages of their booklets. As the teacher (or child) storytells the text, some teachers ask children to tap the page to show where the words *could* go. For example, when Naima wants to write, "I went swimming in the pool," she taps the line where she could write this, moving her finger along the line. In this fashion, children are tapping out the stories to accompany their drawings. This can help children understand that writers eventually record each word with a mark (or series of marks) on the page.

Eventually, once a child has mastered letter-sound correspondence (see the following section) enough to record at least an initial and final consonant in most labels, it is time to encourage children to write sentences rather than limiting themselves to labels. When children first write sentences, many of them tend to produce strings of letters. We can help the child avoid this by asking, "What are you going to write?" Ideally we hope the child will produce one single sentence—we sometimes engineer things so this happens. Then, after the child produces a sentence, we repeat the child's sentence, and as we voice a word, we leave a blank on the child's paper to hold a place for that word. Then we voice the next word, leaving a second slot. We may go back and, pointing to the blanks, "read" the child's intended (and not yet written) text: "I went swimming in the pool." Eventually the child can say what he plans to write, and as he articulates a word, he can leave a blank, in this way setting himself up to write.

Developing Phonemic and Phonological Awareness

Group 1 children of course need to use the writing workshop as a time to become stronger at working with phonemic awareness and phonics. The first challenge will be for children to learn to isolate and hear the initial sound in words. The child may have drawn a picture of the monkey bars and not know how to label them. "Say *monkey bars*," we say. "What sound do you hear at the start of *monkey?*" We need to watch closely to see how the child proceeds. As some children try to isolate the sound at the start of a word, they race past the first sound, stressing the medial or final sound. In this case, we may want to use motor activity to reinforce lessons in phonemic awareness. "Watch my mouth," we say, and shape our lips as if to say *mmm.* Then we'll say, "You do it." And soon we'll ask the child the question again, "What sound do you hear at the start of *monkey bars?*" Once the child has isolated the /m/ sound, we can say, "So write that down." Now, of course, we are supporting the child's knowledge of phonics. If the child does not know how to record the /m/ sound, we can teach the child. Having taught that an *m* represents /m/ on monkey bars, we can ask the child to label other words where this knowledge will pay off: *me* and *Mom*, for starters.

Of course, once the child has written a label for monkey bars (MB) and Mom and me, we will definitely want the child to reread, touching the words as she reads them. If the child reads MO as *Mom*, we may want to highlight the contribution the letters make to reading. Pointing at *Mom*, we might say, "Are you sure that says *Mom?* Might it say *Dad?*" If the child says no, we might add, "How can you be sure this doesn't say *Dad?*" In the end, we might point out, "If this said *Dad*, what letter would you expect to see first?"

Children can often *write* the initial and final sounds for words before they can use those sounds to help them read the words.

Using the Alphabet Chart as a Resource

Group 1 readers will benefit from being encouraged to use the alphabet chart as a resource when they are writing. We will want to teach them how to use this chart, demonstrating that if we want to write *snake*, we say the word, hear the first sound /s/, and then look over the chart, searching for a similar sound. In small groups, we could say to children, "I want to write about my trip to the farm. I am not sure how to write *farm*. Can you help me find the letter at the start of *farm* on the alphabet chart? Let's say the word together. [They do.] Now let's say it again and this time listen for the first sound you hear." Then we can show children how we read the alphabet chart, looking for a picture and a letter that start with that sound.

Soon we can help kids make word associations. If Jeremy knows that the pumpkin on the alphabet chart starts with a P, we can help him think of other words that start the same way.

Recognizing and Using High-Frequency Words

Group 1 readers will need to recognize a couple of familiar high-frequency words. We may want to teach them that, as readers and writers, there are some words they just know. For example, whenever they want to label *me*, they don't even need to stretch out the word and write down what they hear. Instead, they can say to themselves, "Me, I know me. M-e," and then just write the word quickly. We might describe this by saying, "There are words that you sound out,

Supporting
Reading
Development
Through
Conferring in
Writing

∽

94

saying them slowly as a turtle. And there are words you just know, and you know them fast like a rabbit."

Because students will want to "just know" some words that they'll need for their writing, we have the perfect reason to talk up the power of the word wall. It is helpful to gather a cluster of children around the word wall and help them read the word wall words. We might say, "Can you find *Mom?*" or even, adjusting the wording, "If you were writing *Mom* and didn't know how to spell it, where would you look?" We can't assume that children understand what it means for words to be arranged alphabetically!

We want to encourage children to rely on word wall words when they are writing. Sometimes it helps to give children portable word walls that they can keep on hand as they write.

Rereading Using Print, Meaning, and Syntax

Finally, Group 1 readers need to learn that, when reading, they rely on print, meaning (which for these readers often means the picture), and syntax (which means the text should "sound right"). So we want to teach children how to read their own writing, reminding them to rely on all three of these resources. Often young writers have trouble reading their own print, and when this happens we can remind them that it may help to look at the picture or to think about what the book is about. The question, "What would make sense here?" will have special power when the child is reading a story about his or her own life. Of course, because the reader in this instance is also the author and the illustrator, the art will have particular power!

If children read their own writing first in a belabored fashion, we'll want to encourage them to reread it more fluently.

Anticipate Patterns in Predictable Texts

Group 1 texts have highly predictable structures. We want students to use what they know about patterns and language to anticipate what pages may say. We also want them to anticipate what they will write.

You can support the ability to anticipate patterns during writing workshop. Coach your students to reread as they write: Encourage them to first think about the whole of what they want to say ("say out the sentence"). Then as the student writes the first word, she can reread what she wrote and get ready for the next word in the sentence.

Encourage your students to reread their work word by word and then to read with more fluency and phrasing.

You can support this work using interactive writing. In any interactive writing situation, you can emphasize to a larger group of children how to reread to get ready for the next word that will be written. During an interactive writing session/shared writing session (or with a small group during writing workshop), you can use the story of a shared experience to help children learn to anticipate words in the text. Part of the text can be written already. Together, read the part that is written; then ask your students what would come next (for example, half the sentence might not yet be written: *One day the class went . . .*).

We'd now like to jump to a later point in the continuum of reading development so that you may more easily place your own readers along its length.

Helping Group 4 (Level F/G) Readers During the Writing Workshop

When working with children reading at Group 4, developing a wide range of spelling strategies is crucial. You will also be focusing on encouraging students to integrate multiple sources of information and to read with more fluency and phrasing.

Developing Fluency

Have your students practice rereading their writing often. Students are already comfortably nestled within the meaning of the text because they themselves created it. They can work on reading the text with phrasing and fluency to help develop their voice and style. Rereading a piece many times over will also help generate new topics for young writers, help them determine confusing areas of text that need clarification, and help them further develop syntax and grammar. Students might work alone or with partners when working on fluency.

Reading Increasingly Difficult Words by Letter and Word Part

Children can learn to process and read correctly names and words they do not immediately know. For instance, the word *panda* might

*Supporting
Reading
Development
Through
Conferring in
Writing*

❧

96

be read correctly by a child unfamiliar with the animal because he or she is able to process it by letter and word part: *P* + *and* + *a* = *Panda*. In other words, the child knows the sounds made by the letters *p* and *a*, recognizes the familiar word *and* in the middle, and is thus able to read the word.

The following activities may help children practice this skill during the writing workshop.

- While students are writing words (either during a conference or while doing interactive writing with a small group), teach them how to not only hear and record the *letters* they hear, but familiar word parts as well. A child writing the word *panda* could be nudged to write *p* and then the word part *and* rather than stretching out the whole word.

- Ask students to reread their own writing and focus on reading some words by letter and word part.

- While conferring in writing workshop, teach students to use a variety of strategies at once, making decisions about which strategy will help them to spell a word most efficiently.

Using Parts from Known Words to Read Unknown Words

Using known words to read unknown words is a strategy we often use during word study. It is important to assess whether or not students use this and other word study strategies when they are spelling words in their own writing.

Try the following activities to help with this strategy during the writing workshop.

- Coach students as they compose to think about known words that can help them write unknown words. For example, if a child is writing the word *chicken*, remind her that she knows how to write the word *kick* already.

- Do a small-group interactive writing lesson with children who are all reading in Group 4. Focus together on thinking about particular words in this way. For example, in their interactive writing, you might circle three words for which they can use this strategy.

- As kids reread their writing, have them use the strategy of looking at the parts of the word that they know to help them figure out the unfamiliar words.

Using a Variety of Strategies

Encourage children to practice a variety of strategies to spell and write words.

- Circle five words in a piece of writing for which four of the strategies that they have learned might be helpful (stretch out/word wall/known words to get unknown words/letter to word part) and have a discussion with a small group about why each strategy is helpful for spelling each of the words.

- Have students circle five words to work on from their own writing and think about which strategy they could use to solve each one.

- Have students try writing the same word using different spelling strategies and think about which spelling looks best.

- Have students reread their own writing. When they get stuck, you can prompt them to think about what other word they know like the tricky one that might help them to spell it.

Monitoring, Cross-Checking Sources of Information, and Self-Correcting at the Point of Error

As children read more difficult texts (assuming they have been taught to think about what they are reading in Groups 1, 2, and 3), their self-corrections should occur closer and closer to the point of error. In Group 4 we are not so concerned if the child must sometimes reread to self-correct. We do, however, expect self-corrections to *begin* happening at or near the point of error. In this stage we want to teach kids to find their own errors.

- In writing we can reinforce this learning by having students reread their writing constantly. They can do this when they finish the piece and during editing, when they are doing a lot of cross-checking. Also, as they write, students may have points where they stop and reread their writing to check that it makes sense and that it says what they want it to say.

- As children are rereading and self-correcting, they can write words the way they *think* the words should look and then reread them to think about whether they look right.

*Supporting
Reading
Development
Through
Conferring in
Writing*

∾

98

- It is important to use some of the same prompts we use in reading during their writing: Does that sound right? Does that look right? Does that make sense?

- We might get kids to read their writing first like what they want it to say and then again, reading what it actually says.

A child reading at this stage matches the letter-sound patterns in words and reads with more fluency and phrasing on repeated readings of the same text. Here are some activities to support this practice in writing workshop.

- Students can use their writing as a place to work on fluency and phrasing. Have them do repeated read-alouds of their own work. Have them retell their stories and discuss what they want people to learn and what they want to show their readers.

- Have students reread their writing while asking themselves, Does that make sense? Does it sound right? Does it look right?

- Partners can get together to reread their writing, frequently asking themselves, Does that sound right? What is happening here?

Using Meaning, Syntax, and Visual Cues

It is important in reading to identify which source of information students rely on most. When you know, you can support your students in various ways during writing workshop.

- Help children grow stronger in using sources of information they do not often rely on. For example, if students mostly try to sound out words, you can focus in writing workshop on how to use syntax and meaning to write words.

- In writing you may find that students mostly reread and fix spelling errors. This could be their area of strength, which is why they use the visual source more often in both reading and writing rather than syntax or meaning-based clues. Here you will want to encourage students to work on finding parts in their writing to make more clear (using syntax and/or meaning).

- It can also be helpful to teach into your students' strengths. If students are stretching out words in their reading work, you might teach them how to do that better as they write. This will in turn help them do the same work even more smoothly in their reading.

For example, if a child stretches out each letter of a word as he reads *(b-a-n-a-n-a)*, you may want to encourage him to reread his writing in chunks, and to also *write* in chunks *(ba-na-na)*.

Helping All Readers During the Writing Workshop

In this chapter, we have detailed ways in which the work that we do with two different kinds of primary readers (Group 1 readers and Group 4 readers) can be supported during writing time as well as reading time. We could, in a similar fashion, show how this holds true for readers at every point on the reading continuum.

For example, it is important for all readers to realize that their repertoire of known words (such as the high-frequency words on the word wall) can help them not only to read and write those words but countless other words as well. By understanding the principle that readers and writers use what they know to help with what they don't know, children can become resourceful word solvers.

Reading-writing connections happen on every front. Children can learn that as writers, they do not always need to come right out and explicitly say, "I was mad," but that they can, instead, decide to "show not tell." Of course, if the author of a text has shown rather than told something, then the reader of that text needs to infer. By teaching writers to show not tell, then, we are building the same muscles that help them to infer in reading workshop.

When we write, we are constantly "making movies in our minds" and then recording the details of what we see. Reading, of course, is sort of the inverse of writing. When we read, we start with print and use the print to generate movies in our minds—or to help us envision. As we encourage children to "make movies" during writing workshop and to record all of the sensory detail that surrounds the stories they write, we can encourage them explicitly to notice how the good writing that we *read* provides us with the same sort of experience in reverse—when we read writing that is full of sensory detail, as though the writer made a movie in his or her mind, we are able to envision scenarios more completely, we are able to feel as though we have climbed into the world of the book. As writers, then, we want to provide *our* readers with the same experience. This connection, when made explicit, can be very helpful in the context of both reading and writing workshop.

*Supporting
Reading
Development
Through
Conferring in
Writing*

100

When working with students in Groups 2, 3, and 4, we can use writing workshop to support reading work by examining what *specifically* readers are working on within those groups. For example, students in Group 2 (B and C books) tend to be working on using the first letter, recognizing blends, and checking endings. We can teach into these ideas in writing workshop to better support those ideas in reading workshop. In Group 3, children tend to be recognizing chunks and using what they know about one word to help them get another word. We can teach into these ideas in writing workshop as well. In Group 4, children tend to be working on self-monitoring and cross-checking sources of information in order to self-correct. Teaching into this concept during writing workshop will support students' reading work as well.

When working with children at any level of reading, we can study the text characteristics as well as the characteristics of the reader and think about the needs of the students. If we find they need reinforcement, we may look to writing to see how that can help. Using our model for working with either Group 1 or Group 4 readers, we can modify our teaching to address the needs of students reading at all levels in the classroom.

CHAPTER 8

❧

Writing Conferences in Early Kindergarten

By late November or early December in the writing workshop, we hope for conferences with kindergartners that are much like conferences with writers of any age. We hope that our young students have taken on the writing identities that will continue to develop and strengthen as they proceed through their writing lives. We hope they are able to answer the query, "How is your writing work going?" with information about both genre and process, as Theo did one day when he said, "In my story about me and my cousin we made this huge fort out of blankets and I'm adding more details to the part when the fort fell down on our heads!"

We hope that by November, kindergartners will see writing as an ongoing process and count on having time each day to write about topics of their own choosing. We hope they expect, when we approach them for a conference, to be taught something new. They know that writing includes both pictures and words, and that blank paper is transformed by the way they manipulate those pictures and words. They know that writing is for communicating experience, emotion, and information. They know that writers write for many purposes. They know that their writing can be read and understood even when they themselves are not in the room—what magic!

This list of hopes we have for kindergartners in November could be examined as a list of teaching points for the first several weeks of the school year. The truth is, conferring with brand-new kindergartners *is* different from conferring with more experienced writers. Kindergarten is full of "firsts"—not only are we inviting students into a writing community for the first time, but we are also teaching them everything about progressing through a school day for the first time, not to mention moving through the physical space of the classroom. ("We *walk* instead of rolling to our rug spots, Harry.") The beginning of kindergarten is a unique and dazzling time, during which the stage is being set for the rest of children's lives as learners and makers of meaning. It is important to be thoughtful and deliberate about how we set that stage!

Conferences That Teach Expectations for Writing Workshop

Of course, early in the year, management is an issue that deserves all kindergarten teachers' explicit attention. Many minilessons will be devoted to teaching children what happens in writing workshop and what their roles are—just as many early conferences will be devoted to steering children not only toward their identities as writers but also toward their identities as kind and productive community members. During the first weeks of writing workshop, we will find ourselves having many "expectation conferences"—conferences during which we communicate to students precisely what is expected of them during writing time, and help them start doing those things. Later in the year, when the children have learned and internalized our expectations, we hold far fewer such conferences.

It is important to remember that while some of the behaviors beginning writers exhibit can be exasperating and distracting, they are absolutely normal. While *we* have a clear vision of how we want our writing workshop to go (calm, attentive little bodies on the rug, no clamber and rush during transitions, quiet students sitting in their writing spots thinking of stories from their lives and enthusiastically putting them on the paper, etc.), it is important to remember that our students will not share this vision with us unless we teach it to them, step by step. We expect a tremendous amount of focus and maturity from very young people—they are quite able to rise to the occasion, but we must explicitly, patiently, and repeatedly teach them *how*. Our teaching will more successfully find its mark if, instead of responding out of frustration, we quickly and firmly address the issue at hand as if the child simply does not yet know what is expected and we are clueing the child in on it. This is sometimes easier said than done, but devoting conferences to expectation issues early in the year will help our writing community to function smoothly later and will save a lot of frustration and exhaustion down the road.

Expectation Conferences: What Do We Do During Writing Time?

- **Attend to writing and focus on the process.** Early in the year, I confer with Ava about the fact that writing time is for writing and not for rearranging the plastic food in the kitchen center. I confer with Sylvie about keeping her paper flat so she can write on it instead of folding it into a little boat. I confer with quiet Saudin, who is staring dreamily out the window while his paper remains blank. We need to make clear to young learners who really may not understand immediately that during writing workshop, we expect them to write! We want to help them remove any distractions so that they can focus on the task at hand.

- **Share supplies.** I remind Krishna and Erik, when they are trying to squeeze each other off the tiny chair they swear they both sat in first, that a writing community shares supplies and helps each other solve problems. ("Look, there's another chair right next to you!") This is an issue that comes up quite often at the beginning of the year—especially for children who have not had preschool community experiences. If we treat these situations matter-of-factly as simply issues that are getting in the way of children's writing, we can help children resolve their conflicts and get back to work.

- **Learn from compliments.** Simply pointing out what we see going well in the room can encourage children to participate in that activity. This works well when it is a compliment the whole class can hear: "Wow, the red table is already focused on their writing. They all have paper in front of them and are either thinking or beginning to write. Nice work, red table!" It also works well as a more specific compliment at a table where a certain child is off-task. Saying, "I love how you told Tinia so nicely that she could use the red when you were done, Darla, what a great community member you are!" might change Davey's mind about grabbing something from his friend without your having to directly approach him.

Expectation Conferences: What Does *Writing* Mean?

- **Making meaning on a page.** It may take several conferences with some children to convince them that writing (or drawing) is about making meaning on a page. Some kids approach drawing as a kinesthetic activity with little regard for the result on the paper. Early in the year, for example, I worked with Bjorn to help him understand that during writing time, writers draw pictures that show something that *happened* as opposed to experimenting with how fat a dot the new markers might be able to make when pressed down with great force, or what it feels like to scribble as fast as he can.

- **Drawing representationally.** Some children may draw designs or doodles (hearts and stars, pink balloons, things that they enjoy and feel confident drawing) at the expense of recording meaning. Kindergartners may not understand at first that we are asking them to draw on the paper, as best they can, something that happened—which means making what they put on the paper look like what they see in their minds when they think of the event. Helping them to visualize the story and describe it out loud can help them understand what it is we want them to draw. This may be challenging for children who don't feel confident as drawers—then we can teach how writers just "draw the best they can and move on."

- **Putting down letters.** Early in the year, we may not expect very many (or any) of our students to incorporate letters or words into their drawings. As we progress and they develop more awareness of letter-sound correspondence, we do want to make them aware that writers write words to go along with their pictures. This soon becomes more of a process conference than an expectation conference, but I mention it here because children will not know it is expected of them unless we teach them!

- **Using directionality.** It is not unusual for kindergartners to start writing at the bottom of the page and work their way up, or to draw three sequential pages of a story and staple them on the right side. Using the examples found in real books can be very helpful when we want to teach children about directionality: "Look, Leo Lionni always starts his words over here on the left side and then goes across and down." Or "Hold this book. See how we always open books like this, with the closed part over on this side? Your own books should go like that too."

- **Incorporating strategies taught during the minilesson.** While we don't necessarily expect children to incorporate each strategy into their writing processes the very day we teach it, we do expect that, gradually, they will begin trying out things we are teaching in our minilessons. Sometimes kids forget to practice what we've taught or have missed the message of the lesson for various reasons; we can remind them that we expect them to do this.

Expectation Conferences: What Is the Student's Role in a Conference?

- **Respond to us when we ask them questions about their work.** Sometimes young writers don't actually understand what a conference is all about. When we approach and begin asking questions about their writing, not only may they not have a writing plan in mind to discuss, but they may not understand that they are actually expected to have a conversation with us. When I approached Stevie early in the year, for example, he continued drawing the helicopter he saw by Chelsea Piers, humming contentedly, ignoring me completely as I tried to interview him about what he was working on, until I said, "Stevie, honey, look up at me for a minute. Your job right now in this conference is to talk to me about what you are working on. I am asking you questions to find out what you are doing—that's my job—and yours is to answer. So, let's try again . . ."

- **Talk about what they are working on as a writer (and to be working on something).** We definitely need to teach children that we don't just expect them to tell us specifically what they are doing in that moment ("I'm drawing a bunny") but to tell us what part of the writing process they are engaged in. (I'm adding detail to my story about the picnic with my auntie—there's the wild bunny we saw in her yard!") This takes some doing. To answer in this way, children must have been taught some writing process strategies, and they must understand that we expect them to try these strategies.

- **Ask questions if they don't understand you.** Sometimes as we confer with children they are nodding or "uh-huh-ing" away, but when we set them up to try what we've been teaching on their own, we see that they have no idea what we've been talking about. It can be very helpful to teach kindergartners to ask for clarification if they don't understand what we are saying to them. Pausing and saying, "Can you say back what I'm asking you to try?" can encourage this behavior.

Conferences That Elicit Content for Writing

In content conferences we focus on eliciting from our students more elaborate and well-developed stories than those they have begun, and then we help the students start recording those stories on paper. We tend to have more content conferences at the beginning of kindergarten than we do during the rest of the year. This makes sense—the idea that meaning can be represented symbolically is brand new to many kindergartners. They need a lot of coaching to learn how to select meaningful content from their own experience. We must teach them how to express this content orally not only to develop a sense of story and of sequencing but also to simply give them practice with oral expression. Then we need to teach them how to record this content on paper, first with just pictures and then with words as well.

- **Finding a story to tell.** Early in the year, we often find ourselves working to elicit content from children by asking clear questions aimed at helping the young writers bring their stories to the surface. Almost every day during conferring time at the beginning of the year I find myself saying, like I did to Ned when he finally told me about the pigeon that visits him on his bedroom windowsill at home, "WOW, I had no idea! You have GOT to put that in your story so everyone can know about it. How will you start?"

- **Saying more.** After simply getting children to represent any content at all on their papers, the next step is to encourage them to "say more" about it, in the form of adding details or pages to a story. "We went to the park" is not enough. "Say more about that," I told Shanille when she offered that explanation of her story. "What happened at the park? Who were you with?" While we don't want to get into the habit of spending our conferences drawing out details bit by bit—the goal is to teach children that they can ask themselves these questions automatically as they write—sometimes we will want to show children that a story is more than just a brief, nondescript statement.

Focusing on Kindergartners' Drawings

While our goal as teachers of writing is undoubtedly to move our students toward telling their stories by writing words, the importance of children's drawings to their development as writers must not be underestimated. Not only can we learn a tremendous amount about our students' interests, processes, and development by examining their pictures, but the teaching we do into their drawing work is easily transferred to their writing work later. For example, teaching Tumi to add to his pictures only those details that are important to his story about cooking dinner with his mom is paving the way to teach him, later in the year, that writers add to their *words* only those details that are important to their story.

Because at the beginning of the year kids are often more comfortable with drawing than with writing, drawing can be a way to help them become comfortable representing important things about themselves on paper. We want our young writers to understand that the process of drawing—and soon, the process of writing as well—begins with the impulse to make meaning. It begins with "I have something to say." Drawing also provides a physical transition to writing letters.

Look Carefully at Students' Drawings to Learn What to Teach

Children enter kindergarten at many different stages in the continuum of drawing development. We learn where to aim our conferring by looking closely at what they draw and how they draw it.

- **Some children may see drawing as an enjoyable kinesthetic activity rather than as a method of representation or meaning making.** Ambrose, for example, spent his first day of writing workshop vigorously (and with great enthusiasm) swirling an entire fistful of markers around on his paper.

- **Some children may not appear to be drawing representationally.** Stuart, for example, spent his first writing workshop drawing a series of green dots gradually increasing in size across the bottom of the paper.

- **Some children, however, might simply be representing meaning in a different way than we expect.** Early in the year, Basha drew a long and tangled red spiral on her paper. As I conferred with her, it became clear that instead of the meaningless line I initially assumed it to be, Basha was in fact drawing a map—that line represented for Basha "the way to the mountain." Because I asked Basha to explain her drawing, I was able to use the information she gave to tailor my conference with her more closely to her intention. Instead of conferring simply about the idea that writers draw pictures that hold meaning, the conference was about how drawings can do even more and tell a story about something that happened. It is important not to assume what children's drawings mean or don't mean. *Ask* them. They will often surprise us with their unique vision of the world and equally unique method of representing it pictorially. While the goal is to help them draw representationally, it is important to be aware that there is often more meaning hidden in children's drawings than we imagine.

Make Teaching Points About Drawings Transferable to Later Writing Work

It is helpful to use consistent language when we are teaching into, first, children's drawing work and soon their writing work. "Adding detail to your words" will make more sense to kindergartners if they are already well practiced at "adding detail to your pictures." While sometimes, early in the year, our conferences focus on issues specific to drawing, especially with children who are resistant to drawing representationally, we want to make sure that the ideas we teach during the drawing phase of kindergarten writing can be applied to writing as well.

CHAPTER 9

❧

Conferring with Young Artists, Mathematicians, and Scientists

Whether in math workshop, writing workshop, reading workshop, science, or art, the individual conversations we have with children to lift the level of their work, to solidify and nurture their identities as students of whatever subject we are currently studying, are crucial. Transferring what we know about good conferring in writing workshop to other academic areas will not only benefit our students, but will also help us to assess them across different content areas, providing us with a deeper and more well-rounded understanding of each child.

Ideally, our school days are set up so that we *can* do the same kinds of conferring work we do in writing during all other subjects. The specific objectives of our conferences will be quite different after an art or math lesson than they will be after a writing lesson, but the structure and process of our conversations with children will be much the same.

Transferring General Conferring Goals to Other Content Areas

As we think about transferring our understanding of conferring with young writers into other content areas, it is important to first seek out those qualities that are transferable. What are the most basic goals of a conference? If I approach Kenar when he is experimenting with the viscosity of different liquids by pouring them down a Plexi-glas slide, the *content* of my conference will of course be quite different from what I might say to him were he water-coloring over his oil pastel picture of a barracuda, which would be quite different from what I might say were he examining the different parts of a bean seed.

While content will clearly be different and influenced by the academic subject at hand, the general goals of our conferences remain the same throughout the day:

- To lift the level of our students' work and to stimulate their enthusiasm for that work
- To teach one strategy or idea that our students can try out during the conference as we watch, to be incorporated into what they know about being artists, mathematicians, scientists, writers, or representatives of other fields
- To develop our students' identities as mathematicians, scientists, artists, and other kinds of specialists
- To use a predictable structure in order to reinforce both students' independence and our expectations for their participation.

Transferring Conference Structure to Other Content Areas

In any subject area, the conferring process has this basic structure: *research, decide, teach,* and *link.* Certain elements of the structure may be altered to better suit the content we are teaching, but in general, effective conferences follow this pattern.

The Research Component in Other Content Areas

Just as we would during writing workshop, we use this segment of a conference to gather information—not only about what the child is doing (or not doing) at that particular moment, but also about the child's general understanding of the processes we are teaching. We are assessing as we collect information to help make a decision about what to teach.

This may look a bit different during an art lesson than during a math lesson, but the general goals are consistent. For example, approaching Hana as she works on a pencil line drawing of her favorite New York City landmark (which happens to be the Chrysler Building), I first observe her at work and then interview her about what she is doing. I need to hear from her about the choices she is making as an artist before I make an assumption and dive into teaching her something that may not fit her own goals. If I approach Hana and she is drawing a tiny little Chrysler Building in the corner of her vast white paper, my first thought may be to teach her how artists often use the whole paper when they draw. But instead of assuming that my point is the thing that Hana needs most to learn at this moment—just as I would not assume I have picked the perfect writing teaching point from simply reading over a youngster's shoulder—I know I need to sit down and talk to her about what she is doing.

"Hana, what are you working on as an artist right now?" I ask. When she replies patiently that she is drawing the Chrysler Building, I know I need to probe. "I am interested in the choices you are making about how to use the space on your paper, Hana. Can you tell me about all of this white space?" Not only will this clue her in to my assumption that she is making a conscious choice about how to compose her picture (which she may or may not be doing), but it gives her an opportunity to explain her thinking. In this case, Hana tells me that she just likes to draw tiny. After a bit more probing, I see that the decision to draw the building so small was not a particularly conscious choice on Hana's part. I now feel I have enough information about her drawing process to decide to teach her that artists make decisions about how to use the space in their paper, and that in this case it might be helpful to fill the paper with her drawing instead of filling it with white space.

In any subject area, we must give children the opportunity to tell us how they are conceptualizing their own process in order to make informed decisions about what to teach them. In this way we tailor our teaching to the child's own intent, making our conferences doubly powerful.

No matter what a child appears to be doing when we approach (unless it is so far beyond our expectations for work time that we must address the behavior before beginning to confer about process), it is important to find something to compliment before moving on to teaching. This process works consistently to build students' identities as learners, and reinforces specific ideas that we have already taught, encouraging children to continue doing these things in future work. Just as in writing workshop, we need to compliment one thing the child is doing well before moving forward in the conference. For example, when Lukas is drawing a diagram of how he imagines his sprouting seed looks underneath the soil, I might say, "Wow, Lukas, you really have remembered to put in all of the parts of a sprouting seed we've been noticing. I can even see the root hairs! Smart work. Scientists like you know how important it is to notice the tiny parts of things we are studying. Keep on doing that in all of your science work!" The fact that Lukas hasn't yet labeled the parts of the sprout is important to notice as well, and I can hold that in my mind as a possible teaching point, but just as we do when conferring during writing workshop, it is important to compliment him on what he *has* done before moving on.

The Decide Component in Other Content Areas

Just as in writing workshop conferences, the decision phase of a conference in other academic areas occurs quietly, underground. As we make decisions about what to teach our young scientists, artists, and mathematicians, we weigh in our own minds what we have observed in their work and what we have learned from interviewing them. Just as in writing conferences, we must decide on one clear teaching point within the student's zone of proximal development that will lift the level of his or her work, not only for the particular project at hand but for his or her work in general. As we decide on a teaching point, we are simultaneously deciding on the most suitable teaching method— how can I best get my point across and help this child implement the new idea or strategy?

Before examining this next example about deciding what to teach Louisa as she studies seeds, it is important to know a bit about the research that was done first. Through researching Louisa's process as she studies the seeds in the different types of fruit at her table, recording what she sees in pictures on the chart each child in her class is using, I have noticed several things about her work. She is observing the seeds very carefully, working with great focus. She has lined up several different examples in front of her and seems to be moving back and forth between them, first holding the slice of apple with its slippery brown seeds next to the wrinkly, cream-colored orange seed she has pulled out of the orange slice, and then setting both down to pick up and compare the near-invisible seeds of the banana with the huge peach pit. She told me that she is looking at the differences between the seeds and then drawing them on her chart. I have also noticed that she seems to be drawing a picture of each seed in only one of the boxes provided on the chart, leaving the rest of the boxes blank. When I questioned her about this, she said she planned to draw one of each seed in each box. I complimented Louisa on her careful observations and comparisons, letting her know that scientists always do that and reminding her to continue in future work, and then I weighed my options.

In this case, it clearly makes sense to teach Louisa how to use her chart to record in a more organized fashion the excellent observations she is making. I decided to teach through demonstration. In many hands-on activities, this is a wonderful way to clearly explain things to a child. Knowing both my teaching point and my teaching method, I was ready to proceed to the teaching phase, in which I showed Louisa that scientists who are comparing things use each box for a drawing of a *different* thing.

The Teach Component in Other Content Areas

The teaching section of a conference is the point at which we make the teaching moves that we hope will create turning points in our students' lives as writers, readers, artists, scientists, or mathematicians. We also want to tailor the *way* we present these teaching points to the students' processes, using guided practice, demonstration, and explaining and showing an example.

Just as in our writing conferences, the most important part of our teaching occurs when we transfer responsibility for the new strategy or idea to the student. "You try it!" we say, often staying alongside the child to watch her take the first steps into new territory. Whether it is shading an apple so that it looks round or creating complex patterns with snap cubes, the child's own actions inform her learning in a way that simply hearing us talk or even watching us demonstrate cannot fully accomplish.

Guided Practice

Just as in writing conferences, guided practice begins when we decide what teaching point will lift the level of a student's work, suggest he try out the new idea, and then set him up to practice while we coach into what he does. For example, I observed Terrance (after a science minilesson on observing, drawing, and labeling the different body parts of earthworms) gently prodding the end of one of the earthworms in the Styrofoam tray in front of him with the end of his pencil. After interviewing Terrance about his process, I decided to help him put the wonderful observations he was able to articulate out loud onto his paper.

I complimented him on his scientific observations and then said, "I want to teach you, Terrance, how scientists *record* all of their smart observations on paper so that they can remember them and so that other people can learn from them too. You know so many words to describe the parts of the earthworm—anterior, posterior, even clitellum—that's a tricky word! But your paper is blank—it doesn't hold any of your smart thinking. You can draw what you see on the paper, and then use words to label the different parts you know—just like we did with our all-about books in writing workshop!"

As the child tries the new idea (in any content area), we provide support in the form of lean, efficient prompts: "Nice work, Terrance—don't forget to draw the segments, you observed those, too." As the child becomes more confident and capable with the new strategy, we pull back on our prompting: "Great, yes, put an arrow from the word to the part it describes."

Before moving on, we will bring the child back to the beginning of what we taught him and reiterate exactly what he has learned before setting him up to continue on his own: "So Terrance, when I came over to you, you were making some amazing observations of your earthworm, but you hadn't yet recorded any of your thinking on paper. You learned how you can draw exactly what you see, and you've even started putting labels on the parts that you identified. Scientists record their observations on paper so that they and other people can learn from them. Keep that up!"

Demonstration

Demonstration conferences can be extremely effective when we are working with manipulatives of any kind, because we can physically *show* children what we mean. We don't want to be so explicit with our demonstrations that we lead children to do exactly as we do. For example, when teaching Jesse about complex patterns, simply making an ABB pattern with snap cubes, naming it, and telling him to go ahead and make some others like it will not ensure that he understands the concept of complex patterns. We may instead want to demonstrate how to create a complex pattern by making one of our own and explaining our thought process as we do so, and then encourage him to create his *own* pattern that is more complicated than the AB patterns he has become comfortable with.

Just as in demonstration writing conferences, we want to first name what it is we hope the student will learn to do, and then demonstrate how we might go about it (asking the child to pay attention to *how* we do things). Then we explain what we have done, naming what we hope the learner saw. Finally, we help the child to start trying in his own work the concept or strategy we have demonstrated. To carry the pattern example further, I might begin teaching Jesse (after thoroughly researching his process of creating ABAB patterns with the snap cubes and deciding that he is ready to try more complicated patterns) by saying, "You are doing such an amazing job with those patterns—you are really good at repeating a pattern with two colors, like a seesaw! I want to teach you how mathematicians sometimes make patterns that repeat in other ways. I am going to show you how I might make a pattern with more than two colors. Watch carefully, because you're going to try it out soon!"

It is important to remember to stick around and help the child get started on his own work before you move on so that you can ensure that what you have demonstrated transfers into his own understanding. If I demonstrate an ABC pattern and just tell Jesse to try it, I have no guarantee that he has any idea how to practice what he has seen me do. Sometimes getting children to attempt what you have demonstrated requires a bit of guided practice.

Explaining and Showing an Example

When teaching by explaining and providing an example, whether we are teaching personal narrative or painting or the water cycle, it is imperative that we think through our explanation and provide an example that is extremely relevant to what the child is working on. We must, as in all conferences, observe what the child is doing or has done and think carefully about what point will lift the level of the student's work. When we explain, our explanations must be not only explicit but engaging as well—because we are just talking to our students, we must be sure that what we are saying catches their attention and holds it. Whether we are using an example from our own work or from another student or artist, the example must be not only relevant but also accessible to the child. We must help the child see the connection between the example we give and the work that she is about to do. If what we are teaching doesn't fit with the child's intentions and won't lift the level of what she is doing, we've missed the boat.

With practice, explaining and giving an example becomes a powerful teaching method across many content areas. For this method to be effective, we must have a deep understanding of the student as a scientist, artist, mathematician, or other learner. Providing examples and telling children, look, you are just like this artist, or look, you *can be* just like this artist can be very meaningful.

For example, in a kindergarten class hard at work making "mosaic" pictures using cut-up pieces of tissue paper and glue sticks, Won Je was clearly struggling with the gluing process. He seemed to have more pieces of tissue paper stuck to his fingers than were stuck to the paper. As I interviewed him, he said, "I hate art! I can't do it!" and burst into tears. My goal for this conference became clear—to help Won Je know that sometimes it can still be fun to do things that don't come easily to us, a lesson transferable not only to art but to other aspects of life as well.

I decided to teach (after drying his tears) by explaining the idea to him and by providing an example—rather like delivering a miniature keynote speech.

> Won Je, it looks like this project is really frustrating you right now. I want to teach you something—sometimes it can still be fun to do things that aren't easy right away. That's how we learn how to do more and more things in life. I bet when you were learning to walk it wasn't the easiest thing in the world, right? Imagine how many times you must've fallen down when you were practicing. What if, when you were learning to walk, you just decided it was

too hard and stopped trying! It's the same with art, or reading, or any of the new things you are doing this year. Let me give you an example. A boy I know was learning to play the violin. Some of the boy's friends took lessons after school with him, and were just naturally really good at it. But it took this boy a long time to learn any little thing. Lots of times he wanted to quit because it was really hard. But his violin teacher told him the thing I am telling you now—sometimes you can still have fun and learn from something that doesn't come easily. So he practiced and he practiced. Did the boy become an amazing violinist? Well, not overnight. He is still working on it. But the main thing is, he enjoys it, and he wouldn't get to enjoy it if he had just given up. So, let's get you started on this project . . .

Just as with demonstration lessons, we don't want our demonstration or explanation to be the end of things; we want to help the child start working on what we have just taught so that the new concept can be internalized. I helped Won Je, sniffling, to unstick the tissue papers from his fingers and start again, reiterating the point of the conference before moving on.

The Link Component in Other Content Areas

We can deepen our teaching in math, science, art and other content areas if, at the end of a conference, we restate what the child has learned to do and tell her that we hope this becomes part of her ongoing work. Our linking comments are most effective when we restate what has happened not simply in the specific ("So today you learned how to draw a picture of yourself") but in a way that makes the strategy transferable to future work. ("You learned that you can use different shapes like rectangles, squares, and ovals when you are drawing people so that your people look like people instead of sticks.")

Putting It All Together: An Early Kindergarten Math Workshop

Imagine a math workshop on a sunny autumn morning. After a minilesson explaining different ways that children might engage in their first exploration of the pattern block manipulatives (which they will be using in various ways for the rest of their elementary school math education), a class of kindergarten mathematicians works collaboratively in their table groups. Just as how in a kindergarten writing workshop we introduce structures and strategies that will be studied in more depth and complexity throughout children's writing lives, the introduction of pattern blocks begins a relationship with shapes that will deepen and gain complexity as these young mathematicians grow.

I look around the busy room. At the green table, Elisabeth has made what appears to be a beach scene with her pattern blocks, complete with a hexagonal yellow sun and blue rhombus-leaved palm trees. As I watch her fit the red trapezoid over a couple of orange squares to create what looks like a little beach cabana, she stands up and does a small hula dance move before bending back over her creation, utterly focused. At the same table, Alec and Daniel are stacking hexagons. They are competing to see whose stack gets tallest before falling. They move slowly, lining up the edges of the plastic shapes as carefully as if they were building a card house. Collin is making a rocket ship, symmetrical in both shape and color. Sophie and Kayla are making identical flower pictures, watching each other intently. As I approach, I notice Sophie placing a few green triangles right on top of one of her yellow hexagons. She fits them in like pieces of a pie and smiles with satisfaction.

At this point in my math workshop, I am deciding which child to approach, much in the same way that I might observe writers as they begin working before deciding who to confer with. I am thinking about the myriad teaching options I am presented with at just this one table. For example, how useful *really* is what Alec and Daniel are doing? I could encourage them to explore the relationships of different shapes as opposed to simply stacking them. Collin's symmetrical rocketship provides an opportunity to draw *his* attention to the fact that the ship is the same on both sides. Elisabeth's attention could be drawn to the fact that she is putting different shapes together to create a brand-new shape. Sophie and Kayla could be urged to create their *own* pattern block pictures, or I could teach into Sophie's discovery of different ways to make a hexagon. In addition, I am thinking of the teaching options I might have with each individual child.

After thinking it over, I approach Sophie and kneel down next to her. What I say to her will sound very familiar! "So, Sophie, how is it going for you as a mathematician today? What are you working on?"

Just as we do in writing workshop, it is important to teach our students their role in each conference. Sophie knows at this point that her job is to tell me not just about the content of what she's doing, but about the process as well. "I'm working with the pattern blocks," she says.

Now begins a conference that is structured much the same as a conference we might have in writing workshop. My job is to research what Sophie is already doing by asking questions about her process, all the while deciding what I can teach her to lift the level of her math thinking. I will want to compliment her on what she has already done. For example: "Wow, Sophie, it looks like you are doing some interesting things with the pattern blocks. I noticed as I came over that you were fitting some of those green triangles into the yellow hexagon. Mathematicians do that—look at how shapes fit together." When I have gathered enough information and complimented her on something she is already doing well, I will make a decision about what to teach and how to go about teaching it. In this case, I might decide to help Sophie expand her thinking by encouraging her to notice how many ways there are to fit pattern block shapes into the hexagon. Because this is a manipulatives-based activity, it can be very useful to teach through demonstration—a teaching method that fits naturally into hands-on activities. "Sophie," I might say. "Look at the smart thinking you have already done by fitting the triangles into the hexagon. You sort of made another hexagon all out of triangles, didn't you?! Well, did you know that some of these other shapes can be put together to make a hexagon as well? Let me show you . . ."

In this case, because the point of the activity is for Sophie to explore the relationships between the shapes herself, I will not actually demonstrate many different combinations, but I will encourage her to think about the variety of shapes she can use to make a hexagon. Just as in writing workshop, I may follow my demonstration with a bit of guided practice, gradually easing off on my support until I am sure that Sophie understands the new concept. Hopefully her level of enthusiasm for the process will be lifted as well. (I may even want to interrupt the workshop for a moment, as I might do during writing workshop for a midworkshop share, to tell the rest of the class the "cool new thing Sophie discovered" about how the shapes can fit together.) I will reinforce the good work she is doing and link what I've taught her into her ongoing work as a mathematician: "You know, Sophie, any time we are working with the pattern blocks, it is smart to do like you are doing now and think about the way different shapes fit together."

I conferred with Sophie the mathematician in this example, but there would be similar elements to the conversation had I conferred with Sophie the writer, Sophie the scientist, or Sophie the artist.

CHAPTER 10

⁓

Conferring with English Language Learners

Those of us who work at the Teachers College Reading and Writing Project are blessed with the opportunity to work in classrooms filled with English language learners, including many children who are new arrivals to America. I've written about this work in *Nuts and Bolts of the Writing Workshop* and will not repeat myself here, but in this book, Amanda, Zoë, and I do want to answer questions teachers often raise about conferring with these youngsters.

Sometimes when we work alongside teachers, we find that they detour around the English language learner, explaining, "She doesn't speak English." It is understandable that teachers might make this decision. Their logic seems to be, "I have lots of kids and not a lot of time for conferring. Shouldn't I invest my conferring time in interactions with the kids who can understand what I say? The English language learners will learn English by being exposed to it—things will eventually sink in—and once they've got some English, *then* I will confer with them." My colleagues and I try to understand the reasons why teachers sometimes steer clear of their English language learners, because this insight helps us to address these views.

But we also try to explicitly and directly counter these views. It is absolutely crucial that teachers give equal or more time to their English language learners. By conferring with these children and by developing a wise plan to support them in fully participating in the classroom, we can exponentially escalate the rate at which they learn English and integrate socially into the classroom community. At the same time, we can help them learn literacy concepts and skills that they will eventually put to use as readers and writers of English.

I will begin by discussing the broad decisions teachers of English language learners make as they try to develop a supportive context for these students. Then I will zoom in and discuss the ways in which we tailor our conferring so that it is particularly supportive of English language learners.

Developing a Schoolwide, Consistent Approach to Supporting English Language Learners

Over the years, I have come to believe that children profit when the teachers and administrators in a school think about whole-school, systemic approaches to literacy. For example, I think it is helpful to children if teachers at every grade level generally begin writing conferences by asking, "What are you working on as a writer?" or by otherwise trying to learn the child's plans and intentions. Over time, children become accustomed to the fact that they will be expected to tell others about their plans as writers, and they become more and more proficient at doing this.

Similarly, I believe children profit when teachers and administrators across a school think about a whole-school, systemic approach to language. If a school does not seek such consistency, choosing instead to let each teacher decide when she will teach in English and when instruction will be in Spanish, for example, then instruction during a child's kindergarten year might be in English, and first-grade instruction in Spanish . . . or the teacher might shift in and out of these languages as needed. This might sound like an appealing option, but it effectively leaves children always waiting for the teacher to shift into the child's first language.

There is no one right way for teachers and schools to allocate languages, but there is a widespread consensus that children do not profit from being on a different course each year. The decision that a school makes about language allocation must reflect the school's goals for children. If the goal is for children to grow up biliterate, then many people decide to divide instruction so that half of it is in English and half in another language (say, Spanish). If, on the other hand, the goal is for English language learners to become literate in their first language so they can make an efficient transition toward literacy in English, then the division between languages will shift as children become older and/or more proficient, with more and more of the instruction in English over time.

Many schools decide that some components of balanced literacy will be taught in English and others in another language. If this is how language is allocated, teachers tend to begin the year by encouraging English language learners to write in their first language, but they make sure that both shared reading and interactive writing are meanwhile done in English. Over time, this changes so that some month-long units in the writing workshop are in English and some in the English language learners' first language.

Let me be clear. In a writing workshop, continuity is important. Therefore, even in a dual-language school, where instruction usually alternates by day between English and say, Spanish, it does not make much sense for a child to begin writing a small-moment story in English on Monday, and then for that child to add on to the story (or begin a second one) the next day in Spanish. Instead, in the dual-language schools we know best, languages alternate by unit of study or by component of balanced literacy so that the child tends to write for three to four weeks (the length of the unit of study) in one language. If a class is filled with children who all speak the same first language, then it is common for the children to cycle through the same unit of study twice. In other words, first they write all-about books (reports) in their first language; then they write all-about books in their new language. Alternatively, sometimes teachers decide that the most concrete units of study should be taught and experienced in the second language. For example, it is probably easier for children to write step-by-step how-to books than it is for them to write all-about information texts. Therefore, children might do the more supportive how-to unit in English, and the more challenging all-about unit in their first language.

Schools need to develop policies for supporting new arrivals in addition to language allocation policies. Schools that receive many new arrivals might provide children who need extra help with a special classroom, but other times, these children will be brought into regular classrooms where they may need special support. Ideally, new arrivals will have support from a push-in teacher who can help the child understand and participate in the consistent structures of a writing workshop. Often we have new arrivals work as the third in a partnership so the child can listen in and not immediately feel pressured to fully participate. If possible, we link new arrivals with other children who speak the same first language. Above all, it is important that the new arrivals are brought into the social environment of the classroom as quickly as possible.

The First Stage of Language Acquisition: Preproduction or Silent Period

We want to help our new arrivals participate as actively as possible in the writing workshop and the classroom as a whole. Probably during the writing workshop teachers will encourage these children to draw pictures that show their life stories. You may be startled at this idea. "Even if the kids are ten, would you really have them drawing while the others write?" Our answer is that yes, we think there are compelling reasons to invite these children to draw. The first and most compelling reason is this: Above all, we need these children to feel safe enough to begin to participate as actively as possibly in the classroom community.

We want students to make friends in their new community and to feel like valued members of the class. We want them to learn school routines. We want them to be active rather than passive learners. If students know how to read and write in their native language, this can be another important way for them to participate in the class. If they are in the earliest stages of language acquisition in the new language, we may not be able to "read" what they say—but pictures are a universal language. Pictures that accompany writing in the child's first language can provide a concrete scaffold for conversations that student has with us as well as with other students in the classroom community. We can point to people in the picture, asking, "Who is this?" and then attach the name to the person. "Maria," we say, pointing to a girl in the picture. "Is she your *sister?*" Then we can point to the bike. "Is this your [pointing to the child] *bike?*"

It is important to remember that we can in fact assess the literacy levels of children who do not yet speak a word of English. We can learn a great deal about a child by observing her reading and writing work in her home language. While we may not understand Spanish or Mandarin or Tagalog, we certainly can listen to a child reading in her mother tongue and hear whether or not she is reading haltingly or fluently. We can observe her behavior when she comes to a word she does not know and notice what strategies she uses to try and "get" the word. Is she looking at the pictures? Does she point below the word? We can watch for these same things when we ask children to reread their own writing during writing workshop—whether we can understand the child's home language or not.

Simply watching our students who are learning English interact with books can be an excellent assessment opportunity as well. How does the child hold the book? How does she turn the pages, examine the words, engage with texts? We can collect an extraordinary amount of information about them as readers and as writers simply by watching and listening.

Remember that students in the early stages of language acquisition commonly cope by remaining silent. For a period of time, they may not speak at all. It is important to allow their silence, to give it the time and space that it needs.

We can also suggest that the author (of any age) label the drawing—for example, writing *sister* and *Maria* beside the girl. This sort of work is within the grasp of all our English language learners.

Although it is crucial for teachers to interact with these children as much as possible, they need lots more opportunities for interaction than we alone can provide. Most language will be acquired from immersion rather than from direct teaching. We must look for opportunities for students to interact with English. Others in the classroom can take the teacher's place by having conversations about the pictures. It is important to match each English language learner with a peer who will serve as the child's partner. Ideally, of course, the peer speaks the child's first language as well as English. If this is the case, the partner can use the first language to explain the routines and expectations of the classroom. The predictability of a writing workshop is a tremendous boon to English language learners because once the child has learned how she is expected to act on a given day during the minilesson, the conference, the writing time, and the other structures of the writing workshop, then she will know how to act every day.

The writing workshop is also an opportunity to share writing. Of course, if two partners do not speak the same language, the partner will need to do what all of us often do when communicating with someone who speaks a different language. We use pictures and gestures, we role-play what we mean, and we know that the effort to communicate will be one of trial and error.

Meanwhile, during the writing workshop, we do encourage new arrivals to write any way that they can, including writing in their first language. This allows them to participate, to practice their literacy skills, and to have a forum for using whatever they can glean of what the teacher is trying to teach. The fact that the children are writing gives them a reason to pay attention to whatever the teacher is trying to convey. For example, if the teacher is speaking about the importance of direct dialogue, using speech bubbles to show that characters in a story talk, new arrivals can learn this and then make characters in their stories speak. If there is any child in the classroom or the school who knows the new arrival's native language, then it will be important for the author to use this person as an audience.

When we tell teachers that it is crucial for them to confer with children who do not speak English, teachers wonder what this conferring looks like. How do we carry on a conversation with someone in the first stage of language acquisition—someone who may not understand us and who is mostly silent?

The first answer is that we need to remember that many children understand more than they can say or write. It is not so clear that they do not understand anything we are saying. But more than this, if we draw a chair alongside a child, look at and gesture toward the writing and drawing, say, "Tell me about your story," and then wait expectantly for a very long time, the child will definitely understand. He may not understand our exact words, but he will understand that we are interested in his work, that we regard him as a member of the class, and that we expect him to do what the others are doing—including conversing with us about the work. Perhaps most important, he will understand that we want to hear his story. We are conveying all the really big messages even if the child can't decipher one word of English. Better yet, when the child says something and we nod with pleasure and say the word back, registering that we think we understand, the child will feel understood and welcomed.

There are tips for working with English language learners that can prop up our efforts, but we need to remember that, even if we do everything else wrong, pulling our chairs up to sit with these children is what really matters. It is also important to learn from people who know English learners well. These experts will tell you that it is easier for an English language learner to answer a yes/no question or a question that poses two options than it is for the child to give a free response answer. So if we want to give the child maximum support, we might point to the figure in the drawing that appears to be the child and say, "Is this you?" The child might nod. "Yes?" we say. "This is you, Tanya?" Then we point at the picture and say, as if we are reading it, "Tanya." Alternatively, we could have pointed to the same figure and asked, "Is this your dad? Or you? Who is it?" Above all, remember that students in the first stage of language acquisition need to be involved in conversations. They need to have a lot of comprehensible input.

If we ask questions that extend the child's first response, we can find the story behind the child's picture. It is important to synthesize what we learn, saying it back to the child as a story. "So this is your story?" we ask. When the child nods yes, then we can act as if the child has just communicated something (as indeed will be the case) and respond, "Oh! So this is you!" Holding the paper to signal that we are reading from it, we say, "One day Tanya [we point] rode her bike [we point] past the tree [we point] to the park." Then we put the paper down, signaling that we are done reading the story. Some teachers then ask the child to "read" or repeat the story; others don't.

Students often understand more than they are able to communicate, even when they may be in a silent stage. They can gesture, they can often answer yes and no, they can follow some directions, and above all they can learn by listening.

Teachers often ask me, "What if students copy the example that I use in the minilesson or copy another student's writing? Do I tell them to stop or let them copy?" When I respond to this question and others like it, I tell teachers that I generally ask about these situations myself, "Why are they copying my example?" Although it tends to happen in the first stage of language acquisition, this could happen at any of the stages, for the following reasons:

- **We may have not presented or demonstrated a variety of examples.** For the English learners in our classrooms, providing only one model may not be enough to help them latch onto the more abstract ideas in our teaching. Showing students a few different models and giving them the visual representations that convey that this writing can be done with different topics can be very helpful. While I am conferring with a student I may want to demonstrate how to use the strategy with a variety of models or topics.

- **Perhaps the student truly did not understand the lesson.** This may be either because I was not clear or because the student has not acquired enough English to understand what is happening in the lesson. If this is the case, I may work with the student on understanding the minilesson and coach her using her own writing work. I may use the conference to review the minilesson again, using different (or more) visuals and gestures.

- **The student may not have learned that his own experiences are valuable writing material.** Often students are afraid to take risks and may feel that the teacher's example is the only right way. English language learners, in particular, often feel this way. Therefore, it is imperative that we show them the richness in all of their life experiences. We all have experiences to draw upon that are meaningful and significant. English language learners may have a more difficult time *expressing* these experiences, but we must reinforce how important it is that each of us brings our own life experiences to the community.

- **Copying an example may be a way for students to participate and find access to language and literacy.** In this case I may want to confer with the student about how to make the writing more her own. For example, if I made a bike riding story and now the student is writing a bike riding story, I may want to help her make it her *own* bike riding story rather than just copying mine. I may instead want to work with the student to compose together (or in a small group) a new text about a shared classroom experience to give the child the felt sense of writing about a true experience.

- **A student may use the class or a teacher's example as a scaffold to access the language that they have heard and practiced in the minilesson.** In this case I may want to continue this work by helping the student to develop future plans for writing. In doing this, I could practice, develop, and rehearse language that would be needed for his/her future topic.

Remember that every conference is an opportunity for students at each stage of language acquisition to receive comprehensible language input, to interact with the language, and to continue acquiring English in a real conversation. Thinking about our conferences this way will help us to consider the writing development, linguistic development, and next steps that our students need to move forward as readers, writers, and speakers of English.

The Second Stage of Language Acquisition: Early Production

The second stage of language acquisition is what many call the "early production" stage. In this stage, students are beginning to produce English using either one word at a time or short phrases. At this point we don't want to force long sentences. In our lessons and conferences, we tend to ask students either/or questions where the answers are embedded.

In the writing workshop, students can be writing in their native language or drawing images to communicate stories or information (as in non-narrative, all-about texts). Students may label these drawings in English (and write longer texts in their first language if they can). Some may be ready to write simple sentences. Of course, each student is different and will develop at a different rate.

We can confer with the students by prompting them to talk about the content of their writing. We may also want to talk to them about what we notice, naming, labeling, and putting their text together as a story or informational text. ("Oh! So you cook omelets using a frying pan, a spatula, . . .") It is important as we talk with students about their writing to speak clearly and pause often. In this stage, in conferences, we will want to encourage students to include more details in their drawings to develop the setting, characters, and actions. Interacting with the children and with their writing in this way will help to extend their language ability and build vocabulary. We will also want to encourage and teach students how to write cohesive texts that span several pages, even if most of the "writing" is drawing.

Working on phonics and helping children to label their drawings is very important at this stage. Again, working with a partner will be highly beneficial to both students. Partners can

- Read their writing in English to the other student.

- Read their writing in English and discuss in the native language of the partner what it is about.

- Read their writing in their native language to a partner who speaks the same language. That partner can name and label things in English, or perhaps even be able to retell it in English.

- Read the work (or talk about writing) in English (as best she/he can) with a partner who can ask the student questions and add things to the text (either by naming things or helping the partner say more).

The Third Stage of Language Acquisition: Speech Emergence

In the third stage of language acquisition, speech emergence, students often respond and talk in longer phrases and sentences. In the beginning students use mainly present tense when putting together their ideas for writing. It is important to know that the students' syntax is not always correct in this stage. They are experimenting with language and trying to put the pieces together. They may be writing in various ways:

- Students might draw and write their texts. There will be more information they will be able to think but not yet say. Drawing is a way to hold their ideas in a concrete, visual way they can refer to as they write.

- Students might continue labeling their pictures. This allows them to practice and take risks in the spelling of words, which supports their phonological development.

- Students will be writing sentences. We will want to encourage and teach students to reread what they write and to revise it.

We will want to continue modeling and extending the students' language when we confer with them. It is important in this stage to help the student orally rehearse her writing. We may practice with the student by talking about what she wants to say and asking her to say her planned text back to us. We will want to take her words and extend them when we say them back to her. We are not expecting the student to then take *our* words and write them down; rather, we want to model language and help her rehearse what she will write. She may take on some of our language and she may not; both cases are fine.

In this stage we want to help students put words to what they are thinking. We can teach our English language learners (and many other students) strategies that will help them draft their words (using sight words, stretching out sounds and hearing the beginning, middle, and ending sounds). In this stage, too, we will want to help our students learn how to monitor for sense.

Partners can read to each other. It is important to pair the student with someone who is an experienced English speaker. Partners can work on rereading, monitoring for sense, and helping each other try to say more.

It is important for us to keep in mind that each unit of study in a writing workshop puts particular demands on English language learners—and similarly, each unit provides certain learning opportunities. For example, when we are teaching children to write small-moment stories, we can anticipate that English language learners will need help writing in the past tense and using the time markers that show the passage of time. On the other hand, when we are teaching children to write all-about books, they'll need help learning transition phrases such as *for example* or *another reason that.* . . . When we are ultraconscious of the English language learners in our classrooms, then we learn to keep an eye out for them, tailoring our teaching so that we provide the scaffolds they need in order to participate in the same rich, demanding language opportunities that other children receive. Giving our English language learners these supports as we confer will help us teach them how to develop into independent, powerful writers alongside our other students.

CHAPTER 11

✎

Strengthening Your Ability to Confer

I am always impressed by teachers who know enough about the teaching of writing to be concerned about how to conduct more effective writing conferences. These teachers have come to realize that the challenge of teaching a single individual in ways that really matter is endlessly complex. In this chapter, I want to teach you some strategies you can use to get stronger at your conferring.

First, I suggest you think about the big picture of your writing workshop and decide on a game plan for your learning. The decision regarding what you will study and in what sequence needs to be informed by the needs of your class. You may decide, for example, that you need to focus first on developing a curriculum for writing and planning minilessons, and that your focus on conferring needs to wait until you've mobilized the whole class toward a writing endeavor. Or you may decide that your first priorities are to help your students write with more independence and stamina, and to manage a productive workshop. Each of these decisions could involve some work on your conferences, but that work would be part and parcel of another agenda. If you are trying to mobilize the whole class to work on some writing projects, you will use conferences to help you design minilessons that are within the ready grasp of your kids. If you are trying to create a more productive workshop, you may resort to conference fragments only for now.

In general, try to work first on overall, large-scale ways to improve your conferring, and tackle the more focused studies later.

If you decide that your class is sufficiently well managed that you can focus on improving the big picture of your conferring, I suggest you read lots of conference transcripts and try to internalize their structure, language, and tone, just as you might internalize the structure, language, and tone of a story. Don't worry at first about all the little details, but try to see ways in which all of the conference transcripts in this book and/or on the CD-ROM resemble one another and practice predicting what might come next—just as we learn to read stories, relying on what we know of the genre to predict how they will unfold.

Your reading will yield more for you if you give yourself some assignments. Try retelling what happened in general in a conference; this will help you pay more attention to the major moves the teacher makes in the conference. Look at the conferences that match the unit of study your kids are in right now, and look also at those from early in the year, because your conferences should be similar to both of these in some ways. You may first want to note the patterns in the conferences, paying attention to aspects that reoccur. Finally, read a bit of a conference, then pause and see if you can predict how the rest of the conference will go. Try composing new endings (or middles) for conferences. Afterward, of course, you'll want to compare what you've written and what actually occurred in the conference. Remember, sometimes the course we take is an arbitrary one.

When you are working on the big rhythms of conferring, you will want to keep the overall architecture of conferring in mind, making sure that you see the components of a conference as you read the transcripts and that you contain each of these components in your own conferences. It helps to discriminate when you switch from one component to another. Try conferring in front of a friend, saying to each other, "Okay, now I am doing my research" or "I'm going to switch to the link now." Cover the conference architecture, or, if you have it, use the CD to print conference transcripts that do not name the parts of the conferences, and try naming them yourself.

As you work on the big picture of conferences, it helps to think about how teachers move among children, how they sit and how they talk during conferences. If you can, watch a skilled writing workshop teacher at work, either in person or on video or DVD; pay attention to the warm, intimate, yet efficient tone. Notice that teachers sit at eye level with the child, that the child holds the writing, and above all, notice that during a good conference, the child's energy for writing goes up, not down.

Developing Skill at Knowing What to Teach

Once you have spent some time on the big picture of conferring, you will need to decide what will help your conferences the most. Consider whether you want to become more skilled at how to confer or at what to teach in a conference. If you decide on the latter, as many teachers do, then I suggest that you invest time in planning for and practicing your conferences. This may sound odd to you. "How can I plan for conferences when I never really know what children will say?" you may ask, and this question is reasonable. But the truth is, when we plan any of our teaching, we are always anticipating what kids will think and say and do in response.

It is helpful, therefore, for a teacher or a group of teachers to plan their writing units of study by planning not only their minilessons but also their conferences. For example, I know that at the start of the year, some children will draw nonrepresentational pictures. I know some will copy words from around the classroom or write a list of words they know how to spell. Because I know that when I pull my chair alongside children, chances are good I'll encounter both these scenarios, I profit enormously from thinking with my colleagues about how the ensuing conference might go. I suggest that groups of teachers role-play or transcribe possible conferences, thinking together about the array of possible ways to respond.

Chances are good that if you follow our Units of Study for Primary Writing, you will find yourself needing to teach many of the same lessons we have taught in conferences within this book and on the CD. The titles of these conferences are meant to reveal their teaching points. You may want to cluster them and notice the different methods we use to teach "show not tell" or "focus" or "writing with detail" or any other mainstay topic.

You can also look at any minilesson in the Units of Study for Primary Writing series or in your own teaching plans, thinking, "Which follow-up conferences can I imagine giving after this minilesson?" Usually about a third (or as many as half) of your conferences are designed to help children apply the lessons you teach in your minilessons.

Before and during any of your units of study, you and a group of colleagues can pull writing folders from your classrooms and study them. Try categorizing the work according to what it is that you think a group of students might especially need. Say to yourself, "These four could benefit from . . . and these three could benefit from. . . ." You can use an assessment guide in the back of the Units of Study books in our series to remind you of possible teaching points. Or you can develop your own lens to study the writing in the folders. You may look through a writing folder and study how a child elaborates, uses a repertoire of spelling strategies, and so on. You can then develop teaching points and strategies. With a colleague you can practice and role-play through a couple of conferences. You may want to act out an ideal scenario and then try a harder one.

Recruit a colleague to study your children's work and categorize it according to what he or she could imagine teaching. Use your colleagues' ideas to help you realize that directions that seem inevitable to you are in fact choices. Once you have imagined further directions for individuals or categories of students, you still want to approach a conference with an open mind, ready for surprising directions to emerge. However, the prior work will give you a backup plan.

Developing Skill at Knowing How to Teach

You may decide to focus on improving the quality of your conferring methods. To do this, it is worthwhile to study the particular components of conferences, one at a time.

If you study the research component, you will want to do this within a broader study of your children's written texts and of the lines of growth along which children develop as writers. It is fruitful to practice looking at texts thinking, "What was this writer probably trying to do?" It is also helpful to ask, "What do I see here that I could compliment? That I might teach into?" One way to think about what we might support and scaffold in a child's work is to ask, "What can this child do along a particular line of growth?" and "What is this child almost able to do along that same line of growth?" For example, you can look at almost any dimension of writing—say, a child's use of detail—and try to see what the child has learned to do and is almost ready to learn to do. Of course, this question suggests that children's growth occurs along sequences, and this is both true and not true.

When learning to research, you will want to transcribe what you do during the research component of conferences and compare your research to that in the published conferences. Of course, simple comparisons won't be possible because we will be working with different children, and each child will throw different conference curve balls. Still, you should be able to look across texts enough to notice ways in which the research components of conferences differ, and this should prove provocative.

For example, you may notice that in the name of research, you ask a lot of questions about the writer's topic. Look closely and you will see that if we do this, it is generally as part of the teaching component of our conferences. You may notice that your research tends to be shorter or longer than the research components in our conference—and either way, this will be provocative. Often some teachers spend much longer on the research component than we believe is warranted, given the constrained time available.

When you shift to study the teaching component of your conferences, it will help if you realize that this component is almost exactly like a minilesson. Try looking for the replicable moves that we make when we are teaching by demonstration, by guided practice, or by explaining and giving an example. Try to write conference transcripts in which you follow these same moves. For a time, you may feel robotic and scripted, but once you have internalized the gist of how particular conferences (demonstration, guided practice, etc.) proceed, then the learned infrastructure will become just that, and your focus will return to the child and the content of what you are trying to teach.

Writing transcripts of your conferences helps you to see where you start to teach, how you get to hear and watch the student work, and where you spend most of your conference time. By writing and reading and revising them, you begin to revise your teaching.

Once you have studied all of these aspects of conferring, there is still other terrain to explore. For example, my colleagues and I are studying the ways in which small-group strategy lessons are and are not like conferences, the ways we might adapt our conferences for English language learners, and the use of charts and rubrics as concrete reminders of teaching. We are interested in peer conferring and in conferring with a book under one's arm. I believe that you, too, will find the study and practice of conferring to be an endlessly interesting process.

PART TWO

Conference Transcripts

Part Two Contents

A Letter from Lucy Calkins

Dear Reader,

The best part of this book lies ahead of you. In the pages that follow, we invite you to listen in on some conferences that we've conducted with young writers and hear some of the logic that informed our decisions in those conferences. In this letter, I want to share with you how we envision you will read and learn from these selected conference transcripts. If you would like to have many more conferences as well as the ability to sort and manipulate them, we recommend *Conferring with Primary Writers*, the companion CD-ROM to this book.

First, I hope that these conferences will serve as Technicolor, real-life examples of the translation of theory into practice. If you study them, you will see how we take principles and theories of conducting effective conferences into the very real world of classroom teaching. You may be surprised: Perhaps you envisioned that the research component of a conference was more extensive; perhaps you never dreamt that teachers were so explicit and directive. I suspect there will be many ways in which the conferences will surprise you. If you pay close attention to those surprises, it will be as if I've listened in on your conferences and said, "Let me point out some key ways in which our conferences tend to differ from yours." Those differences will not necessarily reveal right ways and wrong ways to confer, but they will provide you with important food for thought.

I hope you look very closely at the conference transcripts. They bear scrutiny. Look across them; compare our conferences and your own conference transcripts, and study the way in which we have done any one thing. For example, what do you see us doing over and over again? Compare the way we tend to give compliments and the way you have done this. You could do similar work with any component of these conferences: research, decide/teach, and link.

You can benefit from categorizing the conferences. I especially recommend sorting them according to the teaching method we use. Are we teaching using guided practice? Demonstration? Explaining and giving an example? Once you have a collection of conferences that use any one of these teaching methods, look at the teaching component in all those conferences and notice what it is we do over and over. You may want to sort out all the conferences in which we try to help kids fill out their spellings, plan, revise, draw representationally, understand the requirements of a genre, or work with partners.

I also hope that these conference transcripts help you plan for the conferring you will likely do within any one unit of study. Sometimes teachers enter into a unit planning only for their minilessons. These transcripts should remind you that you can also anticipate the one-to-one and small-group work you'll probably need to do often within any one unit. For example, early in the year, you can anticipate that you'll need to scaffold your children as they learn to tell and write narratives. During a unit of study on revision, you can expect to help children articulate the revision strategies they are already using. Although the conferences we do with our own children are forever new—in teaching, we don't step into the same river twice—this doesn't mean that we won't benefit from being prepared. The truth is, experienced teachers enter a unit of study anticipating the conferences their children will need. By reading and rereading the conference transcripts, you have a similar opportunity for foresight.

If you are a staff developer (or if you are your own staff developer), you may want to work with these transcripts in other ways. We find it helpful, for example, to ask teachers to cover the labels and work by themselves to divide the conferences into research, compliment, teach, link. The discussion that can follow about what each component is and is not is often powerful. We also find it helpful to show teachers the research component of a conference only and to ask, "In this instance, what might you decide to teach and how would you teach it?" Alternatively, we could show teachers half of a conference and then say, "How would you end this conference?" We might ask, "What might you say to link the conference to the child's ongoing work?" If teachers try their own hands at writing portions of these conferences, they can then compare what they have written with our versions of these conferences. The first three conferences in this collection are fully annotated. We intend for these conferences to spark thinking about how the annotation might read for the other conferences. What might commentary on the remaining conferences point out? What are the generalized steps inherent in the teaching? If you'd like to read annotations for the rest of the conferences, and others, we recommend our *Conferring with Primary Writers* CD.

I hope that after you study these conference transcripts, you become inspired to write down and revise your own. If our teaching is always spoken, then it tends to float away, unexamined. The power of writing is that we take our fleeting words and thoughts, and we fasten them to the page. Then we have in front of us our best-draft thinking, and we are able to say, "Does this match what all of us believe about good teaching?" and "How might we improve upon this?" With transcripts, we can step back from our best practices and say, "So what have we learned about effective teaching?"

My colleagues and I have been talking and thinking about the teaching of writing for decades. The past two years, however, have given us the richest learning experiences in our lives. The secret is that we've begun to put our best teaching onto the page, and to regard what we write as a draft, ready for revision. By reviewing and rethinking what we have done, we are able to clarify and strengthen our best ideas. Amanda and Zoë and I—along with others from our community—have found that by writing down our best practices, we take the first step toward outgrowing ourselves. More than anything, I hope this book lures you into a similar process!

Sincerely,
Lucy Calkins

UNIT 1

❧

Launching the Writing Workshop

CONFERENCES

"What's the Story in This Picture, Nicholas?"

TYPE OF CONFERENCE: Content
METHOD: Guided Practice

Teach a child to represent a story or an idea in pictures.

Research

Observe and interview to understand what the child is trying to do as a writer. In this case, the child is drawing teeth onto a smiling sun.

Nicholas loves to draw. He would be happy to sit with pencils and markers for much of the school day, creating elaborate scenes on his paper. During writing workshop, Nicholas sometimes becomes so focused on the intricate detail of his pictures that he loses sight of the content he wants to convey. After watching Nicholas add a row of teeth to the grinning sun he'd drawn on what looked to be a beach scene, Zoë approached.

    ∽ Remember that a writing conference begins with research, and that research needn't start with you pulling alongside the child. Oftentimes you will want to stand back and watch from afar. Notice the child's engagement, use of materials, and interactions with others. Begin, even from afar, to develop a theory about the writer. In this instance, Zoë had a hunch even before she drew close. She believed that Nicholas often became so absorbed in the colors and designs of his pictures that he would lose sight of the fact that within writing workshop, pictures have a special job to do. The pictures children draw during writing time need to convey a story or teach content to readers.

"Hey, Nicky," she said. "What are you working on? How's writing going today?"

Giggling with delight at his silly sun, he simply pointed at it and said, "Look!" as if certain that she, too, would be amused.

"Tell me the story you are writing today."

    ∽ The detailed teeth on Nicholas' sun support Zoë's theory that this child's pictures weren't preparing him to write stories as much as they could, but Zoë wanted to double-check her hunch and therefore asked Nicholas to tell the story behind his picture.

"Look at the sun. I am making the teeth. Ahhhh."

"That is a goofy sun, Nicholas," Zoë said and smiled. "But right now in our writing workshop, we're drawing pictures that tell the *story* of something that's important to us."

Probe in order to glean more about the child's intentions.

Zoë continued, "What is actually *happening* in your story?"

"Well, I went to the beach, see?"

Name what the child has already done as a writer, and remind him to do this in future writing.

"Nicholas, it is so smart of you to write about a story from your life. Do that all the time!"

> ∾ Notice that Zoë is actually complimenting Nicholas on something he may not in fact be doing yet. She's worried that his pictures are not conveying a story—but he's gestured toward having them convey a narrative and she acts as if this is true and supports it. In this way, Zoë's compliment actually serves to extend what Nicholas is doing as a writer.

Decide/Teach

Decide to elicit oral content. Do this by providing the child with guided practice in telling a sequential story. You will want to be responsive to what the child says by saying back what you've heard and prompting him for more details.

"But did you know that writers first think about what happens in their stories and then they make sure their pictures show those things?"

> ∾ Notice that having taught Nicholas one thing through the compliment (that writers convey true stories in their pictures), Zoë is now extending that lesson in the teaching part of her conference.

Nicholas looked up with a slightly puzzled expression, as if perhaps he *hadn't* quite understood his full responsibility as a writer.

"It's true!" Zoë continued. "Today I want to teach you how writers do that: think about what happens in the story and then put what happens into their pictures."

Help the child get started doing what you hope he will do. In this case, help him tell the story of his text.

"Can you tell me more about what's happening in your picture? I heard you say you were at the beach—but what *happened?*"

> ❧ Zoë's questions set Nicholas up to do what she has just talked about. She's efficient. She knows she has lots of writers who need her attention, and she expects a conference to do a lot of work in a short amount of time.

"Well, I was at the beach with my mom and my uncle," Nicholas said, grabbing a blue marker and carefully outlining the top of the sea.

Interject lean, efficient prompts to scaffold the child's work in a step-by-step fashion.

"Is that you there? What were you doing?" Zoë asked, pointing to the smallest of the figures.

"I was making a sand castle, and then we found the seal."

"WHAT?!" Zoë exclaimed. "You found a seal on the beach? You have to tell me about that!"

> ❧ Each of us knows what it feels like to have someone listen so intently that we find ourselves saying more and more. This active, intent listening is essential in a writing workshop.

Setting down his pencil for a moment, Nicholas looked up and said, "He was hurt I think, and this guy that worked at the beach was trying to help him. He was stinky!" He giggled again, delighted.

"Was he okay?" Zoë asked.

"I think so. He was lifting up his flipper at me!"

> ❧ Zoë would probably have loved to continue chatting about the seal, but she knows that Nicholas has already articulated a lot of content that needs to be added to his text. If she leads him to say a lot more, he could easily be overwhelmed when it is time for him to write what he has said. And so, especially for beginning writers, it is important to make the transition fairly early on between talking about a topic and recording the spoken text onto the page.

Teach the child to record his additional content in a manner that seems appropriate. Take the child back to the beginning of what you elicited through guided practice, and help him get started putting this on the page.

"Nicholas, you absolutely have got to put that into your story! Before we talked just now, I had no idea about all of that important stuff—the sand castle, the hurt seal, the way he lifted up his flipper at you. You are *so* good at putting details into your pictures" (I gestured toward the toothy sun), "but writers work hard on putting in just the details that show *what's happening in their stories*.

> ∾ Notice these words. Over and over, in dozens of conferences, you will find yourself saying "You have to add that" and "I had no idea!"

"So, Nicky, you have a lot of important parts that you need to get into your writing. You have drawn that you were at the beach. What will you do next?"

> ∾ This question is one Zoë will ask often of her children as writers and it makes sense to ask parallel questions now of Nicholas and his drawing.

"I'm gonna do the seal and the seal guy who was helping," he said, drawing a rotund creature near the edge of the water, flippers and all.

Link

Name what the child has done as a writer, and remind him to do this often in future writing. Set him up to continue working.

"That's smart, putting the true story into your drawing. After this, will you always try to have your pictures show everything about your story? Will you put in your sand castle, too?"

> ∾ Nicholas is a kindergartner, and Zoë has decided that for today it's enough to teach him to draw more representationally. If he were older and more accustomed to writing, she'd probably have nudged him to record his story through print as well as pictures.

> ∾ Almost every conference ends with the teacher extrapolating a tip that she hopes can guide the writer not just today but on future days.

"What's Happening in Your Piece?"

TYPE OF CONFERENCE: Process Goals
METHOD: Explain and Examples, Guided
Practice

Teach a child to decide whether his detailed picture will tell a lot about his subject or tell a story about one time, and then help him to record this information on the page.

Research

Observe and interview to understand what the child is trying to do as a writer. In this case, you notice that the child is adding elaborate details to his labeled drawing.

I watched Eli begin to draw his familiar stick figure and then to begin adding the distinguishing features that would turn the generic figure into someone particular. Yesterday his person turned into his mother, with a big curl of hair. Today Eli was carefully adding buttons down the front of his figure's shirt, using just the very tip of a fat blue marker. He had labeled *brother* (BDR), and *shirt* (SRT), and as I watched, he added *buttons* (BTS). I approached.

> ∿ It is interesting to me to notice that often children begin by drawing generic people, and then halfway through the drawing, they seem to decide who the person will be, adding a single distinguishing feature and saying, 'This is . . .' Often the story (if there will be a story) evolves after the person is given a name.

"Eli, how's it going? How's your writing work coming today?"

Eli looked up at me, slightly mystified—perhaps he was not yet equating his delicate work on the shirt buttons with "writing." "Well, this is my brother," he said. "I am putting the buttons on."

"I love his big smile, Eli! Is he your older brother?"

"Yeah, he's bigger than me. He goes to work, and he wears button shirts so I put buttons."

Name what the child has done as a writer and remind him to do this often in future writing.

"Eli, it is so great that you are adding all those details to your picture of your brother. Writers do that. We keep saying more and more; we add on like you're doing. I hope you do this every time you write."

∾ As far as Eli is concerned, he is simply drawing buttons. In my compliment, I renamed this activity for him, "adding details" and "saying more and more." This is significant because I have renamed his activity as something that is a transferable strategy which he can use often. Now, I can say "Do this always when you write." I couldn't, of course, say "Add buttons always when you write."

Probe in order to glean more about the child's intentions.

"I have a question, though, Eli. *What's happening* in your story?" I asked the question as if I could take for granted that Eli's picture represented a story about his brother, although I wasn't at all certain that it did.

∾ This question fulfills two roles. I probe to learn Eli's thinking but also to begin to change it. Here my question "What's happening in your story?" is meant at least partially to remind Eli that we'd talked in class about putting the events of our lives onto the page—a picture of his brother is only a start. A similar sort of questioning might take place when a teacher notices that a child has prematurely declared a piece of writing finished and the teacher goes right ahead and asks, "What are you going to add next?" or similarly, if a child reads what he or she has written and then continues telling more of the story out loud to us (as often happens) we are acting in similar ways if we respond by asking, "Where will you add all that?" as if, of course, the child intended all along to add to the text.

Eli changed the blue marker for a red one and began coloring in the figure's legs. Then he looked up at me and said patiently, "It's my brother."

Decide/Teach

Weigh whether you want to accept or alter the child's current process. In this case, you decide to teach the writer that he can develop his writing either by writing a lot about a subject, or by telling a story about one time. That is, he can write an expository or a narrative text. Teach by explaining this to the writer and giving him an example to illustrate your point.

"Eli," I said. "Can I teach you something? Eli, look at me, buddy."
I waited until he did. "After a writer decides *what* he's going to write
about—and you decided you are writing about your brother—the
writer has to think, 'Am I going to teach people *a lot of things* about
my brother, or am I going to write *a story about one time* with my
brother?' Both choices are good ones. We've read both kinds of books
during read-aloud. For example, in *Do Like Kyla*, Angela Johnson decided to teach *a lot of things* the little sister does like Kyla does. In
Koala Lou, Mem Fox decided to tell a story about *one time* when Koala Lou was in the gum tree climbing contest. Which way will you try
today, Eli?"

> ∽ There are two main ways in which writing is organized. Writers
> can either write non-narratives or expository texts, which in Eli's
> case would probably result in a list-like attribute book in which he
> compiles things he has to say about his brother, or writers write nar-
> ratives. If the child doesn't seem to have an opinion about which or-
> ganization to use, I will subtly steer him toward narratives because
> this will be the focus of another unit of study. In this conference, I
> want to check to see if Eli has an intention of his own.

"I dunno."

Reassess your decision regarding your teaching point. In this case, you
decide to teach a child that writers often focus their writing by telling a
story about one particular time, and then they record that story in a rep-
resentational and detailed picture and in words. Teach by providing the
child with guided practice in doing this.

"Well, Eli, maybe you want to do like your teacher did when she
told about *one time* when she was riding her bike. You could tell
about one time with you and your brother. Okay?"
Eli nodded.
"Then let me teach you how writers do that—focus in on *one
time* and write about that."

Help the writer get started doing what you hope he will do. In this case,
help the child focus on and retell one episode.

"So can you think of *one time* with your brother that you want to
write about today? I will help you put that story onto your paper." I
was quite sure Eli would need me to coach and support him so that he
would understand what I meant by telling a story.

⌒ Notice how I shift from "You must do this" to "Let me help you do this" and then to "Oh, this is such a great thing you are doing." The actual lesson I'm teaching here is not earth-shaking in its importance, but it is important to teach Eli how to learn from what I say and to teach him that "Trying stuff the teacher suggests turns out to be fun."

"Ummmm." Eli tilted his head thoughtfully, squinched up his nose, and gave the ceiling a penetrating glare. "Nope, I just want to draw him," he decided firmly.

⌒ It's important to realize that when a child resists a bit, as Eli is doing, we have choices. We can decide to acquiesce, or we can nudge a bit more. Often a teacher will decide to become more explicit and definitive in the face of resistance.

"Writers do what you do, Eli. We first think of big things we want to write about, and then later we zoom in on . . . we remember . . . one particular thing we want to focus on. What is *one time* you and your brother had together that for some reason you remember?"

"He walked me to school," said Eli and returned to his work coloring in his brother's pants.

Interject lean, efficient prompts to scaffold the child's work in a step-by-step fashion.

"On his way to work?" I prompted.

"Yeah, this morning. He was goin' to work and I was goin' to school."

"Tell me about that walk with your big brother," I said, acting like I would faint if I didn't hear as soon as possible how this thrilling walk transpired. "How did it start?"

⌒ The question, "How did it start?" sets children up beautifully to say—and therefore to write—a narrative that begins at the beginning and progresses through time. Had I only said, "Tell me about that walk to school," Eli would probably have resorted to generic comments about the walk. ("It was nice.")

"This morning, when we were walking, my brother bought us OJ on the corner, and the carton had a hole for the straws."

"This morning your big brother walked you to school. He bought OJ at the corner in cartons that had straws. Then you walked down the street, drinking it?" I reiterated. "What happened next?"

> ∽ When a therapist wants to help a person say more, the therapist often says back what the person has told him or her. "I hear you saying," the therapist says, and this prompts the client to say much more. Teachers of writing are certainly not therapists, but this strategy—active listening, it's often called—works miracles in a writing workshop.

"Well, I threw away my OJ because we got to school, and Justin brought me to here, in our room."

Take the child back to the beginning of what you have elicited through guided practice, and help him get started putting that on the paper.

"I remember that, Eli. But you know something? All that information about how you and Justin walked to school and about Justin buying you OJ on the corner isn't on your paper yet. How will you make your picture and your words show your story?"

"I can draw me there."

I nodded as if to signal, "Go ahead." Eli drew a smaller figure next to the buttoned figure of his brother.

Interject lean, efficient prompts to lift the level of what the child is doing.

"I wonder," I said quietly as if to myself, "what else you will add to show what happened in the story?"

> ∽ Here I'm giving Eli a much lighter nudge to again add on.

Looking over his shoulder at me, Eli added two cartons of orange juice, complete with straws. When he finished, he looked at me for confirmation, but I kept my gaze expectantly on the page. Soon he gave up looking at me and returned to add the pavement under his feet.

"What about labels, Eli?" I asked quietly.

> ∽ Notice that my prompts are lean and quiet. I want to talk to Eli in a voice that he will internalize so that another time, after he draws a picture, a quiet voice in his own head asks, "What about labels?"

Without bothering to look up at me, Eli wrote a capital *O* and a capital *J* right next to the little carton of orange juice he had drawn. Then he began to draw what looked like the school.

Link

Name what the child has done as a writer, and remind him to do this often in future writing. Set him up to continue working.

"Eli, I'm going to leave you now. Keep doing this work of making your story about you and your brother show up in your wonderful pictures and words. Writers do that; we write stories about things that happen. After this, when it is writing time, will you be sure you put the *whole story* on the paper?"

"Writers Share Community Supplies"

TYPE OF CONFERENCE: Expectations
METHODS: Explain and Example

Teach some children that writers share markers during writing workshop.

Research

Observe to understand what the children are doing as writers; in this case, children are arguing over markers.

As Zoë was finishing up a conference with another student, she noticed an uproar at the red table and made that her next stop. Gordon and Sam were halfway out of their chairs—each with a fist holding a blue marker and each doing his best to wrestle it away from the other. Most of the table's marker supply was spread out on the table in front of their seats.

↪ We don't have a need to do a lot of prolonged research in an instance like this.

Decide/Teach

Decide to redirect the writers. Explain to the writers what you expect them to do in a writing workshop. In this case, help the children understand that writing time is for writing, and that a writing community shares supplies.

"I don't see writers working here!" Zoë exclaimed. "Where are the writers, Gordon and Sam?" She knelt between them, breaking their eye contact. "Writers," she said seriously, "*do not* wrestle over markers. Can you imagine Mem Fox and Tomie DiPaola wrestling over markers?"

↪ Trouble can bring out the worst or the best in us and in each other. In this episode, instead of scowling and punishing, Zoë is trying to honor writers and writing time and to call out children's better selves. It's usually wise to attach management to the goal of cherishing precious writing time because the rules and systems exist for the purpose of allowing everybody the opportunity to write, learn, and grow.

"Boys, look at me." They turned. Gordon's eyes were wet and he was breathing hard, little fists clenched. Sam looked determinedly at the floor.

"Writers, I want you each to tell me what is happening here to keep you from your important writing work. Gordon, you first."

"He keeps on taking all the markers, and I need blue! He took all the blues!"

"NO!" Sam interrupted. *"He's* the one taking them! He wouldn't give me any before so I just took them!"

Help the children get started doing what you hope they will do. In this case, help the boys remember that a writing community shares supplies.

"Ah hah. Well, you *know* that I expect writers to be writing during writing workshop, not wrestling. I see that you're having trouble with the markers. I have a suggestion. When we keep the markers in the tub and just take out one when we need it, then *everybody* gets to use the markers. Every writer needs them to be able to add color and details to their pieces!"

> ∾ This could be turned into a lesson on sharing, but Zoë tries to keep the writing dimension of the issue alive, and so she renames their struggle to be all about two children who both want and deserve the opportunity to add detail and color to their texts.

The boys glowered at each other.

"So do that now. Put all the markers back in the tub. Remember, we always keep the markers in the tub and take out just the one we are using. The tub is always right here in the middle of the table so everyone can reach it."

Reluctantly they plopped their hoarded markers back into the tub. As they did, Zoë peered over their shoulders and said, "Look at that—there were a bunch of blues in there anyway!"

> ∾ Zoë had the feeling that temporarily solving the marker issue would not keep these boys focused for the rest of writing time.

Help the children get started doing what you hope they will do. In this case, help the boys sit in spots where they can do their best writing work.

"If it is not working for you two to be near each other today, find a smart spot away from each other."

> ✎ Our job in a conference is to teach the writers, not the writing. Zoë's job here is to intervene in a way that helps not just today but another day.

"Writers sometimes need to move around a little bit to find a spot where they can do their best work. Where would you like to be today, Sam, where you can do your very best work as a writer?" she asked as if there was no other option but to move.

> ✎ It's true that for writers of every age, it's a struggle to make places in our lives within which we can do our best work. Zoë elevates the problem and sets children up to be problem solvers by describing the dilemma they face as a problem other writers encounter.

"I want to be on the rug with a clipboard."

"Good choice. Go get yourself one, and I'll meet you over there in a few minutes to talk about your writing work! Gordon, will you be able to keep working at the table?"

He nodded.

Link

Name what the children have done as writers, and remind them to do this often in future writing. Set them up to continue working.

"So, boys, you're doing a good job remembering that our writing community shares supplies and that we help each other find smart places to do our best work. You can keep these things in your heads every day so that you won't have marker trouble during writing workshop."

৵

Small Moments: Personal Narrative Writing

CONFERENCES

"Can I Show You How to Write What Happened First, then Next, Talia?"

TYPE OF CONFERENCE: Process and Goals/ Content
METHODS: Explicitly Tell and Example

Teach a child to plan and to begin to write a small-moment story that spans several pages.

Talia comes to school excited to tell stories about her weekends, her sisters, and her cats. Her writing, however, often does not reflect the rich detail or content of her spoken stories. As Amanda watched Talia begin yet another picture of her cat, she decided she'd try to bridge the gap between Talia's oral and written stories.

"Talia, what are you working on as a writer today?"

"My cat. Look at my picture of her! She has funny whiskers, and they scratch me all the time."

"Talia, it is interesting to me that you are going back to your cat and writing about her again. Cynthia Rylant does the same thing! She writes a ton of stories about Henry and Mudge, and you write a ton of stories about your cat. You and Cynthia Rylant are alike."

"I love my cat."

"Talia, since we are learning to write true stories right now, I am wondering about how your story will go about you and your cat. Can you remember *one time* you had with your cat?"

Talia stopped for a moment to think. "I can tell *lots* of times. I know all about Desiree! She's really funny 'cause sometimes, sometimes she . . ."

Interrupting, Amanda said, "I know you *could* tell me about lots of times, Talia. But to make a good story, writers choose just *one time*. Can you tell me about just one time with Desiree?"

"Okay. Ummm. Ahh . . . How about when she scratched a hole in the couch?"

"She scratched a hole in the couch? Oh my gosh. You know, you have so many ideas, so right now I want to teach you how you can say it and then write it like a story. I will help you try to think of many things to say. What happened first?"

"Well first, in the kitchen, she was playing with her very favorite stuffed animal mouse. She was funny; she was making funny purring sounds and jumping on and off the couch!"

"Wow! So *first* she played with her favorite stuffed animal mouse. And *then* she jumped on and off the couch and made funny purring sounds?"

"Yep. And then she broke the couch by scratching it, and then she ran away!"

"Were you there when this happened, Talia?"

"Yes, I saw it when she broke it."

"How were you feeling?"

"I was scared. I thought my mommy would say 'No more Desiree!'"

"Talia, can we imagine together what your cat story would sound like in a book?" Amanda quickly grabbed a few sheets of paper from the bins and arranged them into a book.

"It sounds like your first page will start something like, 'My cat Desiree was playing with her favorite stuffed animal mouse. She was jumping on and off the couch and making funny purring sounds.' Quick, sketch that," Amanda said, and quickly, Talia did.

Amanda turned to the second page and looked at Talia. Talia could tell that this was her signal to continue telling her story.

"Desiree was having so much fun that all of a sudden her claws got stuck in the couch. I was scared that my mommy would say, 'Talia, that's it. No more Desiree!'"

Amanda nodded and said, "Sketch something to remind you." When she finished, Amanda turned to the next page, reiterated what she'd said so far, and patted the paper in a way that showed this would be the last part of the story.

Talia continued, "Desiree was scared too. She looked at the couch and ran out of the room. I went to find her." She drew this.

"Wow, Talia, did you know you had so much to write about that one time with Desiree?"

Talia shook her head.

"Here you go. Start getting those wonderful words down on paper. How does it go first?" Amanda handed the stapled booklet to Talia. Amanda wanted to review the story with Talia one last time to make sure that Talia would actually write down the story she had told her, and not the "I love my cat" list of attributes that she had been relying on lately.

"Desiree was playing with her stuffed animal mouse and jumping off and on our couch. She was making funny purring sounds!" said Talia.

"Sounds great. Remember that today and every day, you are writing stories. Whenever you are writing your stories, it will help you to say your story out loud first. Then you can sketch your pictures and write your words!"

Amanda said she would be back later to see how Talia's writing work was going and moved on.

"Can You Reenact That Part in a Way That Shows Me Exactly What Happened?"

TYPE OF CONFERENCE: Content/Process and Goals
METHOD: Guided Practice

Teach a child to dramatize her narrative in order to recall more details.

I approached Isabella's chair and for a minute or two watched as she continued to work.

I noticed that Isabella was continuing to fill in the sky on the second page of a book she'd started the day before. The text said, "I rode my bike." Page two had no words yet.

"Isabella, tell me, what are you working on as a writer today?"

"Well, you see, *this*," and she pointed to her first picture, which showed a bicycle, a tall apartment building, and a girl with blond ringlets and blue eyes on top of the bicycle. "*This* is me on my bicycle outside my house."

"Oh, you rode your bicycle outside your house? What happened next?"

I respond to Isabella's content by repeating it. I knew that by registering that I heard Isabella's story, I would elicit more details. And I knew my prompt, "What happened next?" would steer her toward narrative.

"Well, I didn't write it yet, but on the next page, I fell off my bike and scraped my knee and I had to get a Band-Aid." Isabella made her eyes really wide to accentuate the seriousness of the event.

"You did? Whew. That kind of cut really hurts, doesn't it? You know, Isabella, you have already done such smart writing work this morning. You are really focusing in on one Small Moment from your life to write about, just like writers do. Keep that up!"

"So on this page, you'll draw yourself falling and show how you got the cut?"

"Yup, I'm gonna say, 'I fell. The end.'"

"Let me see if I have the story right so far, Isabella. It goes, so far, 'First, I rode my bike outside my house.'" I turned the page. "'I fell off my bike and scraped my knee and got a Band-Aid. The end.'" I accentuated the run-on nature of the second page, hoping Isabella might catch on to the idea that she could slow her story down a bit.

"Yup, that's it!"

"Isabella, I wonder if the story that you are planning might turn out like Abby's when she wrote, 'We heard the fire drill. We went out. We came in.' You don't have that many details either. Listen." I recited the text Isabella had said she planned to write in a voice that accentuated its bare-bones quality.

"I need to add more details?" Isabella looked rather disappointed that she was further from being finished than she'd imagined.

"Yeah, like the details you all added to the fire drill story. Writers need to tell details or readers can't get a clear picture in their minds of what actually happened. One thing writers sometimes do to get a clear picture of all of the details in their stories is to actually act out what happened. Can I teach you how to do that today?"

Isabella nodded, suddenly curious.

"Show me what happened first."

"I was riding my bike with my mom" she said, holding imaginary handlebars. Then, shrugging, she said, "I just fell."

"Actually *show* me how it happened—think back to what it felt like to be riding and then what it felt like to lose your balance. How did you fall?"

Isabella proceeded to stand up and put her hands in front of her as if she were holding onto the handles. She lowered her bottom and bent her knees as if she was sitting on the bike. Then she turned the imaginary handlebars as if she was making a turn on the bike, and soon she was sprawled on the ground.

"Now I see, Isabella! You tried to make a turn and you lost your balance. You fell on your hands and knees."

Isabella looked at me as if everything I had just said was totally obvious. "Yeah, that's how I hurt my knee."

"Isabella, you just told me some very important details about your story!" I turned her pages back to page one. "I think you better add right here about riding with your mom. On the next page, you can show how you turned and fell on your hands and knees. Otherwise no one will know all that!"

"Can I show it in my pictures?"

"You can make details in your pictures first; that's a good idea. Then put details in your words. I can't wait to hear your story when it is done. Great work."

When I returned later, Isabella had drawn her fall in some detail and had written a long sentence about it. Sitting down next to her, I said, "Remember at first you just said 'I fell'? And then remember how you actually *acted it out!* You thought, 'Wait, how *did* I fall?' and you pretended to fall, only this time you watched and found the right words for it?" I continued, "What you've done today with this piece of writing is what professional writers do. You acted it out— sometimes I do that in my mind—and you found the words to match. Smart work."

"Can You Reenact That Part in a Way That Shows Me Exactly What Happened!"

∾

167

UNIT 3

❧

Writing for Readers: Teaching
Skills and Strategies

CONFERENCES

"Let Me Help You Put Some Words Down, Jalen"

TYPE OF CONFERENCE: Process and Goals
METHOD: Guided Practice

Teach a child who is worried about writing words "wrong" to say a word and then to listen for and record sounds in that word.

I sat down next to Jalen, hoping to watch without interrupting his work. Jalen turned and looked at me as if to inquire, "Can I help you?"

"I'm not ready for you yet. You can keep working until I am."

Jalen picked up his pencil and added to his drawing. Then he turned back to watch me again.

I pretended to be busy taking notes and waited for him to resume work. When he did, I looked over what he was doing and noticed that he had drawn several pages of pictures and written only one word. Had Natalie's recent emphasis on writing conventionally frozen Jalen up? "Jalen, I see that you have pictures on all three pages, and on the first page, you have started to write the words that tell your story. And I notice you aren't writing the words anymore. What's happening?"

"I have a great story. I wrote some of it." Jalen pointed to the one word on his page. "That's the only word I know. I'm stuck. I need help."

"You wrote *I*?"

"Yeah. That's the word I can spell. The other ones have a lot of letters."

"Jalen, you know so much! You figured out that the other words in your sentence have a lot of letters! That is so smart! How do you know that?"

"Well, when I say *basketball*, it's longer than when I say *I*."

"So smart. You are right that when you hear more sounds in a word, that does mean more letters."

"Let's see if we can try to write those longer words. What do you want to write on this page?"

"It's about *I play basketball.*"

"Okay. After I, what word comes next?"

"Play."

"Let's write *play*. Jalen, I have a crazy question to ask you. Are you ready for it? Here it is: Jalen, do you know how a turtle would talk? Would he talk fast or would he talk s-l-o-w?"

"S-l-o-w."

"So when I am writing words that I don't know how to write, I say the word s-l-o-w-l-y, like a turtle, s-l-o-w-l-y. The next word in your sentence is *p-l-a-y*. Say it like a turtle now."

"P-l-a-y. P-l-a-y."

"Good. Now this time, as you say *p-l-a-y* again like a turtle, think about what sound you hear first when you say *p-l-a-y*. Then write the letter that makes that sound."

"P-l-a-y. I hear /p/ and I know a p goes /p/."

Jalen wrote a p.

"Jalen, use the hand without the pencil and put a finger under the p and read what you have written; then say the rest of *p-l-a-y* again, like a turtle. Start with what you have written so far."

Jalen read /p/ and finished saying the word.

"Hear the next sound, and then write the letter that makes that sound."

"I hear /l/ and I need an l."

"Good, Jalen. Do the same thing again."

Jalen read and then orally added on. After he said *"p-l-a-y,"* he wrote an a. Again he said the word *play*. "That's all I hear. I don't hear no more sounds."

"Smart! It is important to listen and to say, 'I don't hear any more sounds.' That means that you have come to the end of that word, and you leave a space (a resting place for no more sounds). 'I play.' You are ready to write your next word. Can you try the next word on your own?"

"I don't know. *Basketball.* It has a lot of sounds."

"Do the same exact thing we did together. It works for longer words too. How about you start and I'll sit here and watch? Say the word like a turtle."

Jalen looked at me with raised eyebrows and wide eyes, but he began "talking like a turtle" and writing down the sounds he heard on his own.

I moved around the room for a few minutes, and then returned to see Jalen still working. Touching his elbow, I whispered, "Jalen, look at you! You can do this on your own! From now on in writing workshop, do exactly what you are doing right now: Talk like a turtle to slow down the word and to hear more sounds; then write down the sounds you hear. Great work."

"Reread as You Write, Noticing White Spaces and Spelling"

TYPE OF CONFERENCE: Process and Goals
METHODS: Demonstration, Guided Practice

Teach a child who has reread and located problems to fix her text and to continue writing, monitoring for spelling and use of white space.

Amanda pulled a chair alongside Nicole, who continued writing, ignoring her. This is, of course, just what she hoped Nicole would do. For a moment, Amanda thought about Nicole and her brothers and sisters. Nicole is the ninth child in a family of thirteen children. As Nicole worked, Amanda read over her shoulder.

Me mi mom wnto thestr.

Nicole finished the text on one page of her story, turned the page, and began to draw on the next page.

Amanda knew she was now interrupting Nicole's independence. "I noticed that when you were finished working on this page," Amanda turned back to her first page, "you went right on to the next page to work on your drawing. Remember in our minilessons how we kept going back to reread? Whenever I finish a page, I definitely go back and reread what I wrote to make sure that it makes sense. Why don't you reread this page?"

Nicole looked at what she'd written and put her finger under the first letter. Amanda saw this and said quietly, "Nice move, pointing under your words."

Nicole's finger followed the print in a one-to-one fashion as she read the first few words, "Me and my mom . . ." At this point, Nicole's text no longer contained white space to demark word boundaries. As she lost track of which letters represented which words, Nicole's finger hovered over her print as she dictated what she hoped her marks conveyed: "went to the park."

"Nicole, can I stop you? I loved the fact that when I pulled my chair up alongside you, you continued working. And I notice you left some spaces between your words. Congratulations. Can I shake your hand, writer?" Amanda gave her a congratulatory handshake. "Leaving spaces like this," Amanda pointed, "is a grown-up thing to do! As you continue writing, you need to keep leaving spaces like these to help your readers."

Nicole nodded but clearly, she was wary. She had become much more independent over the last few weeks and she would be happier now if Amanda left her alone.

"Nicole, I love the way you pointed like this under 'Me and my mom.' Then you had trouble, didn't you? You went like this." Amanda imitated her hovering finger. "You know why you had trouble? Although you put spaces between your words really nicely in the part 'Me and my mom,' in this last part, you forgot the spaces! You could tell that when you tried to read it! That was smart."

"I want to teach you that as you're learning how to make spaces in your writing, it might help you to make lines like these." Amanda pulled out a little portable whiteboard and showed her what she meant. "Then you know what you want to say and have spaces between your words."

"Watch how I make spaces for what I want to write. I want to write, 'My dog and I went for a walk.' Now I need to make the lines that I will write on. Watch!" As Amanda said each word she made a new line, creating dramatic spaces between them to look like the following: ____ ____ ____ ____ ____ ____ ____ ____.

"Do you see? Now I can write my sentence and have spaces between my words. Watch!" Amanda wrote quickly in front of her, saying each word and putting it on the line.

"Let's try to reread yours. When you get to the tricky part, say to yourself, 'What did I want it to say?' And then we will make lines to help you with the spaces."

Nicole read "Me" and then she read "My" and immediately she clasped her hand over her mouth and started to giggle at her own funny talk.

"I bet you said to yourself in your head, 'That doesn't make sense.' Do you need to change it?"

Nicole nodded. "Me and my mom."

"Quick, use your pen to fix it! Use one of those arrows; that's what I do," and she used her finger to show that Nicole could place an arrow between her words so that it acted as a caret. Soon this section of Nicole's text read, "Me and my mom."

"Good. Now reread."

"Me and my mom . . ." Nicole paused again.

Amanda whispered to her, "What did you want it to say?"

"Oh yeah! Me and my mom went to the store! I have to fix it!"

"Great! Let's make the lines now. You want it to say 'Me and my mom went to the store,' right?" The lines went like this: *Me and my mom* ____ ____ ____ ____. "Write the words so the sentence goes like this." Amanda pointed at each line as she said what was already or would soon be written there. "'Me and my *mom went to the store.'* Put each word on its line and reread with your finger and your pen to check it, just like we did, okay?"

Amanda watched Nicole fill in the lines with words, rereading as she progressed through the sentence.

"Nicole, after this, when you go to write, will you first say your sentence and write down a line for each word?"

Nicole nodded.

"So if you were going to write, 'I can leave spaces,' show me on the whiteboard how you'd get ready to write," Amanda said, passing her the marker. Then Amanda helped her say the sentence, "I can leave spaces," while making lines for each of the words. "For a while, make these lines whenever you want to write something, okay?"

"Okay!"

"It will remind you how writers make sure to leave spaces between words so that the words are easier to reread. Let me watch you get started on the next page!"

Nicole turned her page. She stopped. Amanda watched quietly, trying not to jump in too quickly.

"She bought me candy!" She turned her face to Amanda. Amanda pointed to her paper and stepped back. Nicole began to make her lines. She made four lines and started to write.

"What Is the Most Important Part of Your Story, Justin?"

TYPE OF CONFERENCE: Process and Goals
METHOD: Guided Practice

Teach a child to focus on one small moment in his writing; then teach the child to plan the narrative he anticipates writing.

Natalie watched Justin working for a moment, nose poking out of the depths of his sweatshirt's hood, before she approached his table. Gently pulling his hood back (and reminding him, "Hood, Justin, remember?"), she knelt beside his chair. "What is your writing work today, Justin?"

Justin pulled his hood back up over his head and mumbled, "I'm writing my Small Moment of when I got stuck in the traffic jam with my mom." Justin had stapled two pieces of paper together (the big-white-space, four-lines-for-writing variety) and was writing on the second page.

Natalie asked Justin to reread his piece to her, from the beginning. Flipping to the front page and tucking the sides of his hood behind his ears (which then stuck out straight from his head) so that he could see, he read his first page.

> Ones I was siting in a chrarick jam. I was siting their for an hour and
> Then I fimle movd. and then there was a BIG FLOOD it was up
> To four inchis.

Justin's picture showed two rows of cars heading up the page, getting smaller as they got farther away.

The second page reads as follows:

> And then my mom tuk me to the show stor I got snekars and I got
> tennis shows. And I got a fee par of shows their.

There were neither cars nor floods in the second picture. Instead it showed a little figure with arms raised, foot stuck out toward a kneeling shoe salesperson.

"Justin, I am so glad you told me this because I had no idea about that traffic jam or the shoes! Are those the shoes you got that day? They're nice and clean aren't they! Lucky you."

Then Natalie added, "Justin, you have done some smart work here. You told what happened first and next, and you told it in tiny details. On the traffic jam page, you explained how you sat there and sat there and then finally moved. And on the shoe store page, you told about the two pairs of shoes and the free shoes. Telling little details in order is really smart work. A lot of things happened in that day, didn't they!"

"So, Justin, what were you thinking of doing next?"

"I was gonna add that we saw the cousins 'cause we did. We had pizza with the cousins. The water couldn't stop our car."

"I want to remind you of one thing, Justin. Before writers write, we stop and ask ourselves, 'What's *the one thing* I want to focus on today?' We can't write about everything, so we zoom in and write about just one thing. I want to teach you some more about that right now."

"It all happened on the same day," Justin said, poking out his chin. "And my cousins too. I wanna write about it all."

"Justin, I understand that. But this piece is a book of tiny moments. You could make each page into a tiny moment. When we write our small moments, we focus on just one event, one small moment. Later we can write about other moments. Which small moment do you want to write about now? The story of you and your mom stuck in traffic because of the flood or the one about getting shoes?"

"You mean I can write about all of them?"

"That's right. Each one could be its own story! Some of the stories could go in a different book."

"Oh!"

"Remember the other day? Serena's piece was just like yours—full of lots of *different* moments. Her book told about the swings and the bus and lunch at McDonald's. But remember how she decided to take the one page about McDonald's and just write about that? It's kind of hard to choose which moment to write about when they all seem so important, but that's what writers like you and Serena and me need to do."

Justin nodded.

"Let me show you. Which page, which one small moment, do you want to focus on today?"

Justin pointed to the first page and said, "The traffic jam and the flood."

"Justin, this is such smart work, deciding which of your many moments in your piece you want to focus on in a new piece. Writers do that!"

Grabbing a freshly stapled three-page booklet from the bin and handing it to Justin, Natalie said, "Let's plan that story. Remember when we plan, we say what happened first."

"First, me and my mom were driving to the store, and then we got into a traffic jam."

"Can you say more about that, Justin? What did you and your mom do while you were stuck?"

"We were just sitting there and listening to the radio, and my mom was singing."

Opening the blank book to page one, Natalie touched the page and said, "So, *first*, you and your mom were driving to the store and you got into a traffic jam." Turning to page two, she touched the paper and said, "*After that* you sat in the car and listened to the radio, and your mom sang along?"

"Yeah."

Turning to page three, Natalie asked, "What happened next?"

"We saw a lot of water like a lake on the road, and we kept going . . ."

"Justin," Natalie said, as if he had just made an astounding discovery, "do you mean to say that *all of that* great stuff happened in that one small moment of you stuck in the traffic jam with your mom?"

He smiled. "Yeah."

"So let's go back to page one, Justin. You said this page might be, 'Me and my Mom were driving to the store, and we got into a traffic jam.' Yes?"

Justin nodded and started writing. Natalie watched him work, and once he was well on his way, she slipped away. Later she circled back. "Justin, you have a collection of ideas here to make into stories. Always remember to look over your story and think, 'Can I make this into different small moments?' When you have one idea for your small moment, remember to plan it by thinking about what happened first and then next."

"Can I do the shoe store next?"

"Yep. You will need a new booklet for that small moment!"

"I know." Justin nodded, seeming pleased with himself.

Pulling his hood off again, Natalie whispered, "And remember, no hood! We want to see your beautiful and smart head!"

UNIT 4

❧

The Craft of Revision

CONFERENCES

"Make Sure You Are Adding Those Words for a Reason!"

TYPE OF CONFERENCE: Process and Goals
METHODS: Demonstration, Guided Practice

Teach a child that "slowing down" one section and "showing, not telling" are tools to be used for a specific reason.

Oren has been revising a previously published personal narrative about an experience he had at the Halloween parade: When he was dressed as a vampire, someone tried to take his picture. Before Zoë began the conference, she noticed that Oren had already made a few revisions to this text, and now he was rereading his entire draft.

"Oren, how is your revision work going today?"

"Okay. I'm rereading my draft."

"Are you rereading your draft with a specific idea in mind, Oren? Are you getting ready to make a revision?"

"Oh yeah, I'm trying to slow down the important part of my story," Oren said, assuming his role as a writer and adopting the language that accompanied the role.

"What a grown-up writerly answer! You are smart to not just say, 'I am writing about when someone took my picture at the Halloween parade!' but to also tell me what it is that you are working on—slowing down the important part—as a writer! Whenever we have a conference, remember to tell me, just like you did, about what you are working on as a writer."

"When you say you are trying to 'slow down the important part,' what do you mean, Oren?" Zoë asked, even though, of course, *she* knew what the expression meant.

"I mean that I am going to add more words so it takes longer to read it—like the reader has to slow down and read it because there's so many important details."

"Can you show me in your writing where you are doing that?"

Rather than doing just as Zoë asked, Oren read his entire story to her.

I was in first grade.
It was Halloween.
The whole class was in a parade.
I was a vampire.
You know vampires don't like pictures.
So I saw a person taking a picture of me. I said, No!!!!
So the person stopped. He didn't do it.

Oren pointed to the end of the text and said, "Here I want to say more stuff about the person who was taking my picture, because that was the part where I said, 'NO!!!!!' really loud."

"What will you say to slow that part down?"

"I don't really know. I'm stuck. I want to add on here, but I don't know what to add."

"Why is this part important, Oren?"

"Because . . ." Oren paused to think really hard. Zoë gave him time to think. "Well, because I was dressed up like a vampire, right? And vampires are not supposed to get their picture taken ever—something bad happens, but I forget what, so I didn't want the guy to take my picture."

"Ohhhh, Okay. That makes sense. I didn't even know that, that bad things happen to vampires when they get their picture taken! So now you want to add on to that important part so people understand what it was like for you, as a vampire, to see that camera. What you are doing is exactly what writers do! You chose a part that is important; you thought, 'Why is this important? What do I want my readers to know and feel here?' And now you want to slow that part of your writing down by adding on. I hope you always do that. That's really smart."

"So let's get started! If I was the writer and I decided this was the important part I wanted to slow down," Zoë pointed to the page Oren had indicated previously, "I'd reread that bit of the story and try to get a clear picture of what was happening in my mind so that I could remember all of the important details and then write them down. It's like you need to slow the story down in your *mind* first, before you slow it down on your paper. I want to teach you how to do that now—watch me really carefully because I'm going to try it out with your story, Oren."

Zoë began reading from Oren's draft: "I saw a person taking a picture of me. I said, 'No!' He stopped."

"So then I'd say, 'Hmmmm . . . Let me reread that again.' This time, Oren, listen to what I am thinking about as I slow the story down in my mind. I am going to pretend it is happening now. I am going to imagine what I saw and heard: 'We're in the parade, we're dressed up as vampires.'" Zoë pulls her cape around her as she takes on the part and looks over at him as if to say, "Is your cape on?" Zoë continues, "We're in the parade. We round the corner. In the crowd, what do we see . . .?"

Zoë interrupted her demonstration for a moment to say, "See, Oren, I'm remembering all of the things that happened, all of the things I saw and heard—but wait! This is your story—you keep on now, thinking out loud about what you see when you slow that important part down. What happened next? Keep going with the story."

Oren tilted his face into the air and told the story as if in a trance.

I saw a person putting his hand up.
There was a camera in his hand.
I put my hand up. I said, Noooo!

"Good. Do it again, and this time, think about YOURSELF as the vampire. How do they act?" Zoë said in a deep vampire voice, raising her arms up slowly. "Say it like you are writing the story, Oren. Let's start: 'I saw a person put his hand up . . .' Keep going . . ."

Oren continued, speaking as if he was dictating the story: "I put my arms up high in the air. I didn't want to see the flash so I covered my eyes with my black cape. I screamed in a loud scary voice, 'Nooooo!' Everyone started to laugh. I looked out from my cape and smiled, showing my vampire teeth . . ."

"Oh, Oren, this is so much more exciting and clear. Now I understand what was going on when you shouted 'NO!' at the guy. This is so funny."

"Let's get it down on paper. Go ahead and let me watch you get started. Go back to where you first started. 'I saw a person put his hand up. There was a camera . . .' Keep going."

Zoë watched as Oren rewrote the first page. He didn't get every bit that he had said out loud, but his story definitely became more colorful. Before Oren started the third page, she stopped him.

"Oren, this is great work. You decided on a part that was so important to the story that you wanted to revise it and slow it down, and then you reread that part and got a clear picture in your mind of what was happening. Then you sort of acted it out in your mind to remember how it went, what you saw and heard. And now you've already added so much! You really are slowing the writing down by adding words that make your readers understand this part better. Whenever you're revising, remember how it felt to try this out today. I can't wait to read your story!"

∾

"Let's Look at Your Lead and Your Ending"

TYPE OF CONFERENCE: Process and Goals
METHOD: Guided Practice

Teach a child to reconsider her lead and her ending and to use an exemplar text as a source of ideas for improving them.

Lisa stood next to her chair, her legs spread into a wide V, presumably so she could lean closer to her piece of writing, which she stared at intently. After watching for a moment, Amanda approached and pulled up a chair next to where Lisa stood.

"Lisa, you look very serious over here! What are you working on today as a writer?"

Lisa looked up at Amanda, her eyebrows still drawn together from the attention she'd been giving her piece. "I'm finished revising, and I am just rereading my story to see if it makes sense."

Amanda knew that Lisa had been revising her Small Moment story for several days. Lisa had cut and pasted in order to add details, and she had added an entirely new page in the middle of her book as part of an effort to stretch the story out. "Lisa, I can see that you have been really working hard on revising! Would you read your story to me now?"

Lisa read:

> When I was going to plant a bulb I took two gloves for my right hand and my left hand.
> And I took a shovel and I took a bulb.
> I digged it hard as I can. Then I put the bulb in. I dumped the soil back in.
> And I took three more bulbs and buried them.
> I took off my gloves and we went back to our room and our hands were covered with soil. We went to the sink to wash our hands and we went back to the rug.

When Lisa finished reading and looked up at Amanda with an expression of bashful pride, Amanda said, "Lisa, I really liked the way you added all those details about planting your bulbs. I felt as if I was right there with you as you planted, getting your hands full of soil! From this day on, for the rest of your life, are you always going to remember that the way to make your writing better is to reread it and to add more details, like you've done?"

Lisa beamed, and said, "Yup, 'cause now I am six and my dad revises and I do too."

"You certainly do. Congratulations, writer. Can I shake your hand?" Amanda said and gave the youngster a congratulatory handshake. "AND, Lisa, I know you said that you were rereading your piece to see if it makes sense. That is also a super-smart move to make as a writer. What did you decide?"

Lisa gave a little twirl, singing, "It makes sense, it makes sense." She stopped and looked at Amanda. "I think I am done. I am going to write a new story."

"Lisa, you have already done a lot of good work with your piece, and you could stop now. But if you are up for it, I could teach you one more thing that writers often do when we revise our stories. Can I teach you one more thing?"

Lisa nodded eagerly. Revision hadn't caused her any trouble at all and had, instead, won her accolades. She was game.

"When I reread my writing to check if it is the best I can make it, I often check my beginnings and my ends, because they are both really important. I know you already revised your beginning. Are you willing to think some more about your ending? Endings are really important, because they are the last things our readers read. You want to write an ending that makes your reader go, 'Ahhhh! What a nice ending!' just like so many of the stories that we read do. What I do is I reread my endings and think about what works and what doesn't. Then I go to a favorite story and study the ending to see if there is something I could try in my writing.

Can I show you how?"

"I guesssss," Lisa said, a little uncertainly. That was permission enough for Amanda, and she charged forward.

"Let's reread your ending and think about what works in it and what doesn't," Amanda said, and she and Lisa reread the last two pages of Lisa's book.

> I took off my gloves and we went back to our room and our hands were covered with soil. We went to the sink to wash our hands and we went back to the rug.

"I didn't say, 'And then we went home' or 'Then we had lunch.' I stayed in close to that time," Lisa said, referring wisely to a mini-lesson from the *Small Moment* unit in which the class had learned that narratives usually work better if their endings are close to the sequence (and to the heart) of the story.

"You are right. You don't jump from planting bulbs to something *totally* different. But the last page doesn't really feel like it has a whole lot to do with the bulbs, does it?" Amanda mused, rereading it. "So the good thing about your ending is you don't say, 'I went home,' but the not-so-good thing is your ending doesn't really wrap up the story in a way that stays close to the bulb part of the story."

"What I often do when I am trying to get ideas for my writing is I think of other authors who have done what I wish I had done. I am remembering that Julie Brinkloe had one of those 'Ahhhhh' endings. Let's look at it." Amanda retrieved the book and reverently read the ending:

> I held the jar, dark and empty, in my hands. The moonlight and the
>   fireflies swam in my tears, but I could feel myself smiling.

"So let's look at this last page of the book together," Amanda said and began rereading the final page . . . and waiting.

"It says the moon swam."

"You're right. Hmmm . . . I wonder why the moon is swimming?"

"She's crying. Cause the fireflies are gone."

"Oh! And are you saying you notice that she ends the story with her feelings?"

"Yeah."

"Lisa, let's look at your ending and see if you can revise it and end with a strong feeling, like Julie does."

Lisa reread her ending out loud. After a moment, she turned to Amanda with a smile on her face, finger pointing to the sky like she'd just gotten a little lightning bolt of insight. "I know! I can cross out, 'We went to the sink to wash our hands and we went back to the rug.' I can add another page and write the ending how I felt."

"Oh my, Lisa. That is such a smart idea."

"Yep, I'm going to write, 'I walked to the sink and I washed my hands. I hoped that my bulbs will grow.'"

"That sounds great. As you keep working on your writing, Lisa, keep rereading and asking yourself, 'Does this makes sense?' That is always smart work to do."

"Okay!"

"You've done a lot of new things today that you are going to want to do again and again. Remember you can always revise by checking your beginnings and your endings. Think about what works and what doesn't work. This will help to tell you what you need to change. Sometimes it helps to read what another author has done."

"I think I am going to reread another story on my red-dot side and try to revise it again!"

"That sounds like smart writing work. I can't wait to see what you do next with that amazing story."

"Are You Doing Revision Work That Makes Important Changes?"

TYPE OF CONFERENCE: Process and Goals
METHODS: Explicitly Tell and Example, Guided Practice

Teach a child to mentally reenact her vignette in order to add significant details.

I pulled my chair alongside Annabelle. Anticipating my interview, Annabelle quickly looked up and said, "I'm revising."

"Great, Annabelle. How'd you know I was going to ask about that?! Can you show me how you have revised your piece?"

"Well, I added in right here and here and here," Annabelle said, pointing to a bow she'd drawn on a girl's hair band, to the word *very* she'd inserted into a sentence, and to a phrase she'd tucked onto the end of one page.

"Hmmm. Did you work on revising another story before you started working on revising this one, Annabelle? I forgot."

"Yep. See here," Annabelle said, pulling out the piece she'd revised previously. "I added, 'I was glad,' and I made grass and I said what kind of dog he was."

"Two things please me about what you're doing. I love that you can show me the revisions you've made, Annabelle. It looks like you have thought to yourself, 'What else can I add to my drawing and my writing?' And I love your energy for revision. I guess you are the kind of writer who is willing to work hard to make your best work even better! Annabelle, whenever you revise, always remember to ask yourself, 'What else can I add to my writing to make it better?'"

"Annabelle, I want to teach you more about revision. I see that you have made some changes in your writing. You have added a hair bow, a letter, and a few words. These are small changes."

"But revision is about making big changes that make your writing a *whole* lot better. There are lots of techniques or tricks writers use to make our writing A LOT better."

"One way to get important details into your story is to act out parts of your story and think about what you are doing. Then you find words that help create a picture in your readers' minds."

"See, you have the plan, the outline, for a very nice story here, but as soon as you begin it, it's over. The way you wrote this would be as if Mem Fox wrote *Koala Lou* by saying, 'One day a koala bear was in a gum tree climbing contest and she didn't win.' You and I are really glad that Mem Fox didn't leave out about how Koala Lou climbed faster and faster, thinking, 'I'm going to win and my Mom will wrap her arms around me and say, "Koala Lou I do love you" . . .' and we are glad Mem Fox told about the people waving their party hats and cheering. You need to add *those* kinds of details to your story. I will show you how."

"What I do when I want to tell more is I reread my story and act it out or imagine it in my mind. Would you reread the first page or two with me and then watch how I try to act out this part of your story?"

Annabelle opened to this page and read aloud.

I piket up the prazint. I watid to opin.

"Let me picture it!" I responded and then reached out for an imaginary present. "So you picked it up," I said. Now the imaginary present was on the table between us. I peered at it as if trying to guess what was in it. "Hmmmmm," I said. I repeated the words Annabelle had given me, speaking slowly and suggestively. "I picked up the present . . ." I again reached my hands around the imaginary present as if to feel its weight.

"Hmm, I wonder what else you could add . . ."

Catching on, Annabelle added, "It was kind of heavy. I really liked it; it was so big."

"Show me how you picked it up. I was just guessing."

"I couldn't lift it. It was so big," she confided.

I looked at Annabelle's page and said, in astonishment. "Where did you write that?" Then I added, "This information you are telling me is so important, Annabelle. You definitely need to add on that it was heavy and you kind of liked it and it was so big. Where will you add that?"

Annabelle pointed to the obvious spot, on the bottom of her page. Soon she'd added sentences onto the first page of her book.

I piket up the prazint. I watid to opin. It was hava I cidit likee it.
It was sow big.

"Smart. On this page, you had lines that were empty. If you didn't,
you could always staple on more paper."

"Keep going. Reread and act it out."

Annabelle found the next page and reread what she'd already
written:

and then I piud the sting.

She gestured with her hands as if she was pulling the string off the
imaginary present in front of her and meanwhile repeated the words
on the page. When she finished saying them, she looked up as if she
knew her sentence ended midstream and said, "And the paper came
off!"

"You think that'll help people picture what happened?" I responded, containing my excitement so I didn't overpower her.

She nodded.

"You are a fast learner. Keep going."

Before long, Annabelle's second page looked like this:

And then I piud the sting. The raping parlu fat opf of the prazint. I
cappy the sting and I cappy the bow wae.

"Annabelle, do you realize that your revisions are as long as your
book was? You have made HUGE revisions. And now you have a
strategy for revising anything you write. You go to the first page and
read it, like you did today. As you read that page, go back in your
mind to the event you are writing about and sort of act it out; get the
whole thing happening in your mind like a movie. You will remember new details just like you did today."

I got up to leave and realized that Annabelle was not writing. "Let
me watch you keep going."

Annabelle looked at me. She reread her writing. "I kept the string
and the bow . . ." She held her hands out as if holding the string and
the bow. I stood up slowly and began to step back, looking over her
shoulder. I waited for her to start writing. Annabelle stuffed her hands
into her pockets. She turned around and said, "I put them in my
pocket!"

"Write it down. Keep going, Annabelle!"

"Are *All* of Your Words Important to Your Story?"

TYPE OF CONFERENCE: Process and Goals
METHOD: Guided Practice

Teach a child not only to add on but also to subtract in order to develop his main idea.

Pat looked around her room, thinking over which child she'd approach next. Aziz caught her eye. She saw him taking more paper. She was excited that he was adding on pages, but knowing Aziz as a writer led her to imagine that he might need help with this process. She wanted to support his decision and effort by teaching into what he was doing.

After observing Aziz for a moment, Pat asked, "What are you working on as a writer today, Aziz?"

"I'm adding pages to my story about going to Canada. We went to the Canada Hotel, and I was sleeping when we got there."

Pat glanced quickly at his piece, noticing what he'd written so far.

"You are adding pages? Did you add some of these just now?"

Aziz nodded. "This, 'I went to my sister's house,' and this, 'I went to my bed,'" he answered, referring to his last pages.

"Aziz, I love that you have written a long story with so many pages, and I love that you are revising like a real author. Congratulations. Authors do what you do—we reread our stories and add on. Do this all the time."

Aziz nodded, happy. "It's nine pages!"

"Aziz, I'm proud that you are revising—so proud, in fact, that I think you are ready to learn another important revision strategy! You are getting really good at *adding on* to your stories, but another important strategy that writers use when they are revising is to *subtract* parts that don't fit or that aren't important to the story. I want to teach you about that today, okay?"

He nodded dubiously, and Pat forged ahead.

"See, Aziz, the question a writer needs to ask himself is this: 'What is the most important part of this story?' After he knows this, then he can reread his piece, thinking about what doesn't belong with the most important part and then just cutting those parts out. So let's try it—what is the most important part of this story?"

"It's that I couldn't go swimming. And it was hot."

"Hmmm. Well, if the swimming is the main part, I am wondering why you chose to add on a whole different thing about your sister's house instead of adding on about the swimming. Does the part about going to your sister's house have anything to do with the story of not being able to go swimming?"

"Not really."

"That happens to me! I add on . . . and then I realize I added to the wrong part. When writers revise, we sometimes end up taking out pages that are not important to the story. Which pages do you think you need to take out? Can you show me right now?"

Aziz pointed to the pages about going to his sister's house and going to sleep and about eating breakfast. "These ones."

"Yeah. As a reader, I agree with you. You can just rip those pages off and then add on the important stuff you meant to say about swimming instead. Easy as pie!"

"So, Aziz, you've done important and tricky work today. It is hard to take away something that you worked hard putting on paper, but you have realized that sometimes the best revision strategy is to subtract, or take out, the parts that don't fit or that aren't important to the main story. And now, Aziz, you could still add on, like you know how to do—but whenever you do that, you'll want to add things that fit with the most important ideas of the story. Why don't you reread your piece again to see if you could add on to the important part?"

Pat wisely decided to stay and watched as Aziz got started, just to be sure he understood what they discussed. He did, and she moved on.

UNIT 5

∼

Authors as Mentors

CONFERENCES

"What Is the Most Important Part of Your Story, Marley?"

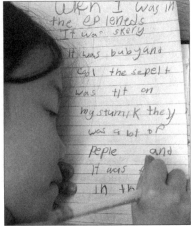

TYPE OF CONFERENCE: Process and Goals
METHODS: Explicitly Tell and Example,
Guided Practice

Teach a child who has written a long many-moments story to focus on the most important part; then teach the child to elaborate on the important part and plan what she will write.

Amanda pulled a chair alongside Marley and watched as she continued to write without looking up. Marley had filled almost one page in a four-page booklet (each page contained many lines and no space for pictures). Anticipating that Marley might have difficulty maintaining focus with such a long text, Amanda intervened. "Marley, you've filled up a long page! What are you working on as a writer today?"

"I am writing about my friends Danielle and Gabi, and I'm telling *all* the stuff we did! We did a lot of stuff!"

"So when I asked, 'What are you working on as a writer?' are you saying that you are trying to cover all the things you guys did together?"

"Yep. I want to fill up all the pages!" Marley said and watched as Amanda read the story. In it, Marley talked about going to Danielle's house and then Gabi's house, teasing Gabi, playing cards, wanting to have a sleepover, and finally having a sleepover another day with Danielle.

"Marley, you have done some good work here remembering all the things you have done. Remembering what happened helps to put a picture in your mind and find details. I love your energy for writing. Keep it up in all your writing!"

"Marley, you have told about so many different things here. Sometimes writers first put a lot of things on the page, and *then* we say, 'Wait a minute! I wrote one page about ten different things. I should probably decide which one thing I really want to tell about.' Then writers can zoom in on one particular thing like we've been talking about in class."

"Can we try that? I am wondering which part of *your* story is the one most important thing you *really* want to write about?"

"When I was playing with Danielle and then my dad came. We wanted to have a sleepover, but we couldn't because it was a school night."

"Do you see the important work you just did, my friend? You first wrote lots of things, and then you said, 'Wait a minute. I wrote ten things on one page!' and you made the smart decision to zoom in on one key moment. Like writers do, you decided to focus on just that moment, at the end of your play date, when your dad arrives and you said, 'Please?' That is a beautiful small moment . . . don't forget from now on to ask, 'What's the most important part?'"

"Let's use another booklet to write this small moment. Let me see you touch the pages and plan what will go on each page."

"This page is us playing."

"When you plan, say the exact words you might write."

"I heard the bell. Oh no, it's dad. Then dad came in," Marley said, and then turned the page. "Pleeeease, can I have a sleepover?" Turning to the last page, she said, "This page will be my dad taking me home."

"Sounds like a good plan. You need to write that." Returning to page one, Amanda read from her transcript of Marley's plan. "On this page, will you write, 'I heard the bell. Oh no, it's dad . . .'?"

"Marley, do you see what you've done? You have planned your story out, saying the exact words as you touched each page. Now you are writing! Keep us there in the moment when you were begging and your dad was deciding. You have to make us wonder, 'Will you be able to have the sleepover or not?' like in *Joshua's Night Whispers*, 'Will he find the night whispers or not?'"

"Okay. Yeah, I can make you wonder!"

Amanda stepped back to make notes in her pad. As she looked up to see where to go next, she saw Marley's head was down, her long curls shading her face, her elbows spread out, and her hand writing.

Amanda returned to Marley after she had finished another conference to check in with Marley's progress.

"I like what I am seeing. You are really staying in the moment! See, you got this one moment out of this page that had like ten ideas. Whenever you remember a small moment, you want to think about which part is the most important! And then plan your story! Okay?"

"Yeah, I think I am going to do swimming with Gabi and Dani at the beach."

"Remember to think about the important part!"

"When we made sand castles!"

"Keep working, Marley. Good plans!"

"But How Did You *Feel* in Your Story?"

TYPE OF CONFERENCE: Process and Goals
METHOD: Demonstration

Teach a child to emulate an author and to show feelings.

Allison is writing on a piece of paper with long lines on it. She sees Amanda standing near and ducks her head back toward her writing in a hurry.

"Allison, what are you working on in your writing today?"

"I'm trying to write about a feeling like Angela Johnson did."

"What do you mean?" Amanda asked, pulling in closer so she could see Allison's writing.

"I went to get my ears pierced, and I was scared. I thought it was going to hurt."

"Angela Johnson *did* write about feeling scared in *Joshua's Night Whispers.* You are right! Do you remember how she did this?"

"Joshua was in his bed with a scared look on his face. Like here in my picture. I am scared. I am on my dad's lap."

"How else did Angela show Joshua was scared?"

"The way he moves slowly down the hallway."

"How did you show it in your story?"

"My dad was there. I sat on his lap when they did it. I thought it was going to be a needle."

"Yikes! Is that all here in your writing? Do you slow down the part about the needle?"

Allison looked down and was quiet, and then she looked up at Amanda.

"Not exactly," she said, looking morose.

"So why do you look so discouraged? You've done some great work already! Good work, author. Let's see." Then Amanda touched one finger as if to start a long list. "You zoomed in on the Small Moment when you got your ears pierced—starting when you sat on your dad's lap." Now, touching a second finger, Amanda said, "You decided this is really a story about being afraid, and you wanted to build up that feeling so we readers would be shaking in our boots, just like you were." Touching a third finger, Amanda said, "And you realized Angela had done the same thing in *Joshua's Night Whispers* when she shows him being really afraid."

"You are doing really important work as a writer; you've got your job all figured out! You're trying to show your fear, like Angela did. Do you have an idea how you can do that?"

"I could add, 'I was so, so scared.' Right here, I could say that."

"You could. Good writers try to make their readers feel by slowing down part of their writing and building up the feeling across pages."

"Like show, not tell!"

"Yes. I think you need to build up the fear part by having it on many pages so readers get scared and more scared. Remember when Joshua was scared and Angela had him walk past one thing, another, another . . . and only at the very end was he safe with his father? You need to bring your fear out over your pages too. Watch. I'll show you how I might stretch out the scary part in your story and visualize it as I go."

"What I do is remember what happened, step by tiny step: I went in, I sat there with my dad, the guy comes, he says whatever he said. Then I think, 'Which was the scary part of this story?' I imagine if it was me, it might have been the needle! So I'd zoom in on the part about the needle. Listen how I might slow that down: 'I was sitting on my dad's lap, holding his hand tight. I saw the needle coming. I closed my eyes tight. I didn't want to see the needle.' See how I said a lot about that one scary part? You try now."

"The needle was coming. It was big and long."

"Oooh! That sounds good. And scary!"

"I can add more! 'I squeezed my eyes tight.'"

"Quick! Add it before you forget!" Allison went back to the start of her story and reread it. When she reached the place where she sat on her dad's lap, she reached for extra paper.

"When you are trying something out like an author, it helps to revisit that text. Let's have *Joshua's Night Whispers* right next to you as you write. You will be trying to stretch out the part about being scared over the next few pages of your story. When writers really try to help readers feel something they were feeling in their stories, they often stretch that moment when they had the feeling and write down all the details—like Angela does, and like you are about to do! You can do this often in your stories."

"I am going to do that in this one too!" Allison pulls out another story from her folder.

"Great idea. But first, let's work on this one. Okay, Allison, as you get started with adding your feelings, I am going to go confer with Zack. When I come back to check on you, be ready to show me parts where you have stretched out the scary part."

"Can We Study What This Author Did and Let Her Teach Us Some Lessons?"

TYPE OF CONFERENCE: Process and Goals
METHOD: Guided Practice

Teach a child to look to authors to learn the power of adding precise details.

Liam sometimes sits and sings to himself with his eyes focused on some faraway point in the distance. Zoë has learned through experience that this does not necessarily mean that he is being unproductive. Sometimes he is thinking through how his writing work will go that day; sometimes he is simply imagining what he and Miles will do on their playdate. Usually, however, the bit of time Liam spends looking into the distance before he starts to write seems to be productive. As Zoë watched, Liam suddenly flipped open the story he had begun yesterday and began working, as if someone had tapped him on the shoulder and said, "Get started."

"Liam, I see that you are working on the piece you started yesterday about your country house. How's that going?"

"Good. See, I'm just coloring my bedroom. Look, it has so many shelves!"

"Ahh, yeah, I do see. Are those your books up there in the squares?"

"Yep."

He continued working busily.

"So, Liam, I'd love to hear your story from the beginning to see how it's changed since I saw it before. Can I read it?"

"Sure."

Liam turned to the front of the book and Zoë read.

I went to my country house. (I WN to MOE KoChRE HAOS)
This is my garden. (thIS IS MOE GORDI)
I like my living room. (I LUK MOE LIVnRM)
I like my bedroom. (I LUK MOE BeJRUOMO)

"Liam, what a wonderful and interesting choice you have made in this piece. It looks like you have zoomed in on one topic, your country house, and then made each page tell about *one part* of your country house. This page is about your garden, this is the living room. Writers sometimes organize their pieces just like you did! Another cool thing about this piece is that you don't have other pages about school or your friend's house. Every page stays on the topic of your country house. It reminds me of Angela Johnson's *Do Like Kyla*. She doesn't have other pages about her mother or her school, and your booklet is the same."

"What are you thinking of doing next, Liam?"

"I was gonna write about basketball 'cause I played it last night. I just gotta color this in first."

"I'm so surprised that you are planning to just go on to the next piece of writing! How odd—why wouldn't you want to revise this piece?"

"It's almost done; that's the reason," Liam said, coloring furiously. "Just as soon as I color this . . ."

"But, Liam, you know when writers really care about pieces they've written, they don't just whip through them and move on to the next. They spend some time making sure that each piece is as good as it can be. So I can tell you care about this piece from the way you talk about it. Let's try again. What's your plan for this piece?"

Liam shrugged. "Well . . . I don't know what to do."

"Oh! *Now* I understand! That happens to me too. Sometimes I am like you and I *want* to make my writing better, and I'm not quite sure how to go about it. Are you saying you want to revise this but need someone to give you ideas for how you could do that?"

Liam nodded. "If you tell me how to change it, then I will."

"Let's see . . . one way to fix a piece is to go to a friend or a teacher and say, 'Can you help me?' But sometimes writers don't have teachers beside them and so they need to make their own teacher. Can I show you how to make yourself a teacher?"

Liam giggled and suddenly started acting out that he was engaged in a construction project, bent on building a teacher.

Zoë ignored the hammering gestures and kept talking. "The way we make a teacher for ourselves is that we find an author who can teach us. And Angela can definitely teach you. *Do Like Kyla* is a lot like your book. Remember how she doesn't just tell about one moment she had with her sister but she lists *many* moments she has with Kyla?" Zoë begins to flip through the pages, reminding Liam as she goes. "She and Kyla wake up, and they eat breakfast; she and Kyla go outside and make footprints and snow angels, she and Kyla go to the store. There are lots of different parts, right? Just like you have lots of different parts: 'I like my living room. I like my bedroom.'"

"Yeah, we both tell a lot of pages, and I'm going to add the kitchen."

"Let's read one of Angela's parts together and see if she did anything else you want to try as a writer."

> Got me some purple snow boots like Kyla, and we both crunch,
>   crunch in the snow all the way to the store.
> Past the big store window, I see myself.
> I do like Kyla and skip past the window, watching . . .
> In the good-smelling store Kyla asks for cheese,
> A bag of apples, and a jar of jam.
> The man in the white apron says, "Goodbye and be good."
> I do like Kyla and say, "OK, I will."

"What are you noticing that Angela does, Liam?"

"She doesn't just say, 'We go to the store,' she tells more stuff like it smells good, and they got jam and all."

"So try that, Liam. Like here, on page two. What details can you add to show what you do in your garden?"

"I just weed with my mom, and I play with my tractors in the rows." Pointing to his picture, Liam said, "Here's the rows, and there's the carrots, but they're still under the ground."

"So are you thinking that maybe you'll be like Angela and add in that in the garden you weed and play tractors in the rows? That's beautiful. Will you add on to each page to show what you do in all of these places?"

"Sure."

"Okay, why don't you get the tools you'll need to do this important revision work?" Liam headed off to get paper, scissors, and tape to add on to his story.

When he returned, Zoë said, "So, Liam, I'm so excited to see what you decide to add to each page, saying what you do in each place. What a great idea, to try out something that Angela does. What are you going to add in here, on the page about your living room?"

"Ummm. It has sofas?"

"Okay. Or you *could* say what you and your mom *do* there, like you did on the garden page. It's up to you. Let's tape paper here at the bottom of the page, and you'll have room."

"Liam, this is so cool. You are writing a Many Moments piece, just like Angela did in *Do Like Kyla,* but you made yours into a list of different rooms in your country house. Now on every page, you are adding in what you *do* in each of the places you write about. What page will you add to next?"

"The one about my living room. I play blocks in there sometimes."

"Great, Liam. Keep going!"

∾

Nonfiction Writing:
Procedures and Reports

CONFERENCES

"What Are You Teaching Your Readers?"

TYPE OF CONFERENCE: Process and Goals
METHODS: Explicitly Tell and Example,
Guided Practice

Teach a child that writers of how-to books draw pictures that match their writing and teach their readers something about their subject.

When Zoë approached Damien, he was very intent on his drawing. The can of colored pencils was close by his side, and he was carefully choosing the colors he was planning to use and laying them out on the table. Zoë noticed that his pages were filled with words as well.

"Hi, Damien, what are you doing as a writer today?"

Damien, familiar with this question, responded matter-of-factly, "I'm coloring my picture."

Because she still needed more information before she could decide how to best help Damien, Zoë repeated his response, encouraging him to elaborate. "Oh, so you are coloring your picture . . ." Her intonation signaled that she was sure he'd now provide details about his process.

"I'm drawing a picture of me driving a car. This is my car and I am going to put me in this part of the car and I am going to put my sister here and my mother over here and my father over here," Damien said as he pointed to the different places in the car. Then he added, "One time I went for a ride in my car with my family."

"But, Damien, what does your piece teach us to do?"

"How to drive a car, see?" Damien pointed to the text of his book, which did in fact provide instructions for how to drive a car.

"Hmmm . . ." Zoë said, looking at the picture. "So, Damien, let me see if I have this straight. You are writing a how-to piece to teach us how to drive a car, and you decided to use a picture to help teach your readers how to drive a car. Am I right?"

Damien nodded a bit uncertainly. It seemed to be dawning on him that Zoë's words had implications for his writing work. He was beginning to anticipate the direction Zoë was taking.

"Damien, I'm not convinced that this picture helps me drive a car."

Damien looked at his drawing, again uncertain.

"It's a great picture if you are writing a story about one time when you and your family went for a car ride, but this is a How-To book, right?"

"Yeah, I wrote all about how you do it! I mean, *I* don't really know how, but my mom and dad do!"

"That's great, Damien. But today I want to teach you how writers of How-To books work hard to make their pictures match their words, Okay? Your drawings need to give us information that goes with your book. For example, let's look at the book I made, *How to Do Yoga*—see?" Zoë put her book down on the table in front of Damien and flipped through the pages. "I used diagrams to show specific poses and materials. If you want your picture to really be a good helper to your words, then you have to make sure that the picture that you draw gives the information that you want it to give."

"Oh, yeah, you have the picture of the 'warrior' pose," Damien points out.

"And I have an arrow pointing to the knee because it's bent. It is important that people know to bend their knees."

"And you have an arrow at the arms showing how they go too."

"Exactly. So let's do that with *your* writing. Go back to all this great work that you have here. Read it aloud so you can really hear the words."

Damien proceeded to read his piece. "How to drive a car. You get the keys. You open the door and then put the keys in the place on the wheel. You turn the keys." Suddenly Damien stopped and looked up.

"What's up, Damien? Why are you stopping?" Zoë asked, somewhat surprised.

"It doesn't match!" Damien said, smiling.

"Say more. What doesn't match what?" Zoë prompted.

"Can I get a new piece of paper and make another picture?" Damien asked, ready to get down to business.

"Sure, you know that you can always take more paper. But tell me what you are thinking."

"This is not a helper picture," he said, crumpling it up.

"What are you thinking of putting in your picture so it can be a good helper?"

"I'm going to make a picture of me putting the keys in the steering wheel and putting on my seat belt, because that's what I said over here," he answered as he pointed to the first few steps in his writing. "And then maybe I'll make another picture for these other words."

"Damien, this is a really helpful thing to do in all your writing. You want your pictures to support your words and give important information. Your readers will be learning from them as well. So maybe after you work on this piece, you could work on others. You can re-read your directions and make sure that the picture matches the information in your words."

"Which Part Goes Where?"

TYPE OF CONFERENCE: Process and Goals
METHOD: Guided Practice

Teach a child that writers can re-sequence their writing by cutting it apart, reordering the steps, and gluing it back together.

Laurie watched Lindsay from a distance, noticing that she had her writing laid out in front of her and seemed to be reordering the pages in first one fashion and then another. After observing this for a bit, Laurie decided to move in and talk to her.

"Hi, Lindsay. What's the writing work you're doing today?"

"I pretended that I was making my omelet to see how my directions worked, and I made a mistake, but I'm not sure how to fix it." From Lindsay's intonation, Laurie could tell that she welcomed assistance.

"Before I pulled in to talk with you, Lindsay, I stood over there and watched. I couldn't help but admire the work you were doing. You had your papers out, and you were rereading and thinking and moving them one way and another and doing the hard work of trying to solve your own writing problem. I watched you and said to myself, 'Now there's a *writer!*' When you find that there is a hard part, you should always try and fix it like you are right now." As Lindsay beamed, Laurie added, "Do you want to keep working on this on your own, or do you want to see if I can help?"

"I want help."

"So can you explain to me what's causing you trouble right now?"

"I wrote in this box, 'por [pour] the egg into the pan,'" Lindsay read from a paper. "And I wrote here 'macks the egg wath a for' [mix the egg with a fork], and that's not the right way."

"Can you say more? What do you mean that it's not the right way?"

Lindsay quickly answered. "I need to change this," she said, pointing to the words and the pictures alongside them. "I forgot. You have to mix the egg *before* you put it in the pan. I don't know how to put these words over here."

"Lindsay, are you saying that when you reread and tried out your directions, you noticed that your omelet recipe didn't work, and now you want to change the sequence, the order, but you are not quite sure how you can do that? Is that right?"

Lindsay seemed relieved that Laurie had understood the problem.

"Lindsay, do you remember when we talked about revising by cutting and adding strips and taping our drafts?" Laurie said, signaling the piece of shared writing that they had worked on as a class during the previous unit of study. "You can do the same thing with your how-to paper. When writers want to change the order of something, they often cut their steps out and then reread their steps to tape them together the way they want them."

"Let's try and do that together with your piece of writing. First, show me the part that is in the wrong place." Lindsay obligingly pointed out the section of her draft that was out of order.

After looking over the section, Laurie said, "So here are some scissors. See if you can't solve the problem on your own. I bet you can!"

As Lindsay looked up at Laurie questioningly, scissors in hand, Laurie simply nodded kindly, encouraging the young writer to take the leap on her own. She knew that Lindsay had done this kind of work before and would simply need a bit of nudging to do it again in the context of her directions.

Lindsay used the scissors to separate her page into little slips of paper, each representing a step. Once the steps were separated, she seemed to be at a bit of a loss as to how to reorder them. Looking at the many strips of text with great determination, Lindsay sat very still.

"You could reread what you've got there, Lindsay. Think about which one should go first. Then switch around the part you thought was out of order. Remember about mixing the eggs before they go in the pan?" Laurie whispered, not wanting to interrupt Lindsay's focus.

Slowly Lindsay started moving the strips around until she had reconstructed her text in the appropriate sequence.

Watching her, Laurie said, "I love the way you are rereading your piece again and again to make sure the decisions you are making are smart ones."

Lindsay leaned back from her work and eyed it, tongue poking out with concentration. When she looked up, signaling she was satisfied,

Laurie suggested she reread the whole thing and make sure it made sense and felt smooth.

"Lindsay, can you tell me what you just did?"

"I cut out the steps in my writing and put them in a new order!"

"You sure did."

"And then I read them again. And now I'm gonna glue 'em back together."

"Before you do that, are you sure that there aren't steps you want to add in?"

Lindsay read her how-to one more time to be sure.

"What a smart thing you have done! You had a tricky problem and you solved it! Keep working out the hard parts of your writing. Always remember that writers keep scissors nearby. If things are out of order or you want to add a new step in, you can always cut and tape."

❧

Poetry: Powerful Thoughts in Tiny Packages

CONFERENCES

"What Does the Rain Remind You Of?"

TYPE OF CONFERENCE: Process and Goals
METHOD: Guided Practice

Teach a child to use comparisons to see the subject of his poem in a fresh new way.

Owen likes to write about water. He writes about the beach; he writes about the swimming pool and the bathtub. He spends an inordinately long time at the classroom sink— long after his hands are clean, he stands staring at the swirl of water down the drain, face calm, oblivious to the bottleneck of children in line behind him. He has been working most recently on a poem about the rain. As Zoë watches him settle in, he picks up his pencil and rolls it back and forth in his fingers. He looks not at his paper but up toward the ceiling.

"Hey, Owen, how is it going for you as a poet today?"

"Pretty okay. I'm writing about the rain."

"Oh yeah, I remember you started that piece yesterday, right?" Owen nods. "So what are you planning to work on today?"

"Well, I want to make it sound better. It just sounds like a boring story right now."

"Why don't you read it to me?"

"Okay. 'The rain streams down the streets. We play in the puddles.'" He looks expectantly up at her.

"I love that great word you used, 'streams.' It makes such a clear picture in my mind. You didn't just say that the rain *goes* down the street; you used a word that shows exactly how the rain was going. That is so cool—you are really thinking like a poet!"

"Now," Zoë says, getting serious, "what was that you were saying about feeling like your poem is boring? Can you say a little more about that?"

Owen looks hard at his paper, shrugs his little shoulders, and says, "I don't know. It's just not exciting."

"Hmmmm. I am wondering something, Owen. Do you mean that you want your poem to look at the world in a fresh new way? Have you been remembering the poem about the pencil sharpener, how it says that there are bees inside of it? And how Ronia wrote that day that the piece of wood was like a little boat for a mouse? And how Toby wrote that the seashell was like an ear? Are you thinking that, like these writers, you want to see the world like a poet?"

Owen nods vigorously. "I said my shoe was like a wagon for my gerbil!"

"Yeah, I remember that!"

"Owen, poets sometimes have to spend a little while thinking really hard, focusing in on the thing or idea they are writing about, in order to come up with brand-new ways of describing it. Do you think you could try to think about rain in the same way that we thought about your shoes that day?"

Pointing to his first line, Zoë says, "Why don't you start up there, at the beginning, and reread that first line? How could you think about that rain streaming down the streets in a brand-new way so you can say it like no one has ever said it before?"

Owen rereads the line, scowling deeply with concentration, and then all of a sudden his eyebrows shoot up nearly to his hairline. "It's like when I play tic-tac-toe, the way the streets are! The rain goes down the streets like someone is playing tic-tac-toe!"

"Oh my gosh, you are right! The streets *do* line up like a tic-tac-toe board. And the rain running down them is like a dark line. Owen, do you realize what you just did?" Zoë asks solemnly.

"What?!" he asks, equally as solemnly.

"You described the rain on the streets in a way that nobody ever has before. You are thinking like a poet. You *have* to write that down, right now! And, Owen," Zoë says as he begins to write, "you know, you can do this ALL the time when you are writing. Poets often go back to poems that they have already started to see if they can use a comparison to see what they are writing about in an even fresher way. Your job today is to find another place in your poem where you can do what you just did with the part about the rain on the streets. I'll come check on you and see how that goes, okay? Great work!"

"What Is the Most Important Feeling in Your Poem, Klara?"

TYPE OF CONFERENCE: Process and Goals
METHODS: Demonstration, Guided Practice

Teach a child to write a poem using concrete detail.

I watched a group of children from afar, noticing that they all seemed to be writing brief little poems that didn't have a lot of depth. I figured if I could get one of the children to reinvest in his or her poem, then I could use that work to make a larger point in either a strategy lesson or a minilesson. I was unsure of which child I wanted to work with first, but just as I watched, Klara looked up. She seemed to have just finished a poem called "Moon."

"So, Klara, what's up?"

"I just finished this poem. It's about the moon," she said, and I quickly read the poem.

I love when
The moon is full
And a little bit when
The moon is half

Then she added, "My next one will be about Sandy because she is my half-aunt and half-cousin."

"Klara, it's interesting how your love for the moon is big when the moon is big and then smaller when the moon gets smaller. A lot of people write about the white moon in the sky, but I have never seen someone write about the moon in quite this way. I can tell you have tried to look at the moon in a fresh way. That is important when you write poetry. You are off to a good start."

"Yes, and I am done," Klara said, and opening her folder, she added this poem to a big pile of others. As she did this, I scanned her folder and noticed that she'd produced a huge number of small poems that each began with the words, "I love . . ." I found this a little troubling: I love gummy worms, I love ice cream, I love weather, I love the ocean. Her folder was bulging with them. I had an image in my mind of Klara as a little poetry mill, feverishly churning out poems without taking time to reflect.

"Klara, I was just peeking at your poems in your folder, and the one thing I notice is that you often begin writing with a strong feeling. You have written about lots of things you love—the full moon, the gummy bears. It is wise to write about topics that matter to you."

"Klara, I want to teach you one thing about writing poetry. This is one very important tip: You need to show, not tell. Do you remember how we learned earlier that instead of saying Poppleton was furious at Cherry Sue, Cynthia Rylant *showed* us how mad he was. She had Poppleton grab the garden hose and start spraying right at her! Well, instead of telling us that you love the moon when it is full, or gummy bears, or anything, you need to *show* us that love and not just tell us."

"So, for example, Klara, what I would do is to imagine I am looking up at the full moon and get those feelings of loving the moon inside me, and then I would show you exactly what I see and notice. Watch me: 'I was looking up, and I noticed . . .' Now I have to think about why I love it. Let me fill myself up with the feeling! 'The moon . . . it was round and I could see the bumps and craters on it!' I thought, 'The moon is so big, watching over us at night!' Maybe in my poem I would write, 'Moon/big and round/glowing with craters/ keeping us safe at night.'"

"That sounds pretty."

"Thanks, Klara, but do you see how I show you what I love about the moon? I imagined myself looking at the moon, and then I really filled myself up with the feeling of love."

"Yeah!"

"Right now, can you try that? Would you remember one particular time when you noticed the full moon? Get it in your head, okay?"

I waited while Klara seemed to leaf through her memories. After a bit, she nodded as if to say, "Got it."

"So what happened? What do you see?"

"Me and my mom saw the full moon, and it was . . ."

"Tell me more. What did you notice?"

"It was like a full moon and it was glowing down at us." Then she added, "I said, 'Look, Mom,' and then we walked . . ."

"Can I interrupt? Stay with the moon. What exactly did you see? What did you think?"

"I was thinking it looked like a *D*. And the other day, it looked like a *C*."

"Klara, you absolutely must put that down on the page. You need to tell about looking up at the moon with your mom and how it looked like it was glowing down on you two . . ."

Klara began writing quickly. When I returned, Klara had added to her poem.

I love when
The moon is full
And a little bit when
The moon is half

I know something
About the moon

When the moon is
Like a D
It is growing bigger
When the moon is

Like a C
It is getting small

"Klara, this makes such a stronger picture in my mind than it did before. I want you to remember what you just did: You imagined the moon and what happened in your mind and then you thought about what exactly it is about the moon that you love. And look, you have words now about that! You can do that whenever you're writing a poem, and you can do that when you revise some of these other poems too."

"Should I keep writing this poem?"

"I think you have more to say!"

"Like write about it glowing?"

"Beautiful. Then you can look in your folder and try it with another poem."

"My aunt poem?"

"I think so. You will have to think about a time with your aunt and fill yourself up with the feelings you have for her to show us!"

"I can do that!"

"I know you can."

Index

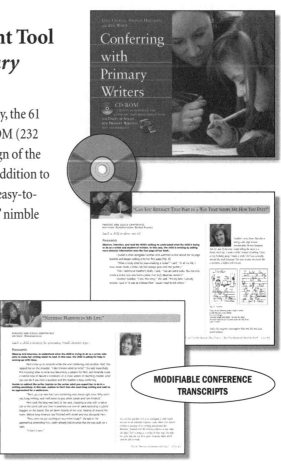